THE JESUS LIBRARY

JESUS AND POWER

THE JESUS LIBRARY
edited by Michael Green

JESUS AND POWER

David Prior

HODDER AND STOUGHTON
LONDON   SYDNEY   AUCKLAND   TORONTO

Unless otherwise stated, all scripture quotations come from the Revised Standard Version.

British Library Cataloguing in Publication Data

Prior, David
    Jesus and power. – (The Jesus library).
    1. Bible. N. T. – Gospels – Criticism,
    interpretation, etc. 2. Power (Social
    sciences) – Biblical teaching
    I. Title   II. Series
    226'.0832   BS2555.2

   ISBN 0 340 39084 0

CONTENTS

ACKNOWLEDGMENTS

Over the last three years I have discussed the theme of *Jesus and Power* with innumerable people, mainly in London and Washington DC. Reading and talking around the subject have consumed more time than actually writing the book. There must, therefore, be countless insights, comments and perspectives which I owe to others. I want to thank all the individuals and groups who gave me time and hospitality, several at great personal inconvenience, especially Steve, Nancy and Matthew Skancke and their *au pair* Elaine Pickering.

An initial draft of the manuscript was read by Michael Green, the series editor, and Andrew Hodder-Williams, then of the Religious Books Department at Hodder and Stoughton. Both made invaluable and constructive comments, many of which have been incorporated in the book. I would like to thank them both for their insights.

I particularly wish to thank Clare Garrett, my secretary, who moved from the House of Commons to the house of the Lord at St Michael's Chester Square. Within a year she has learnt to handle a new parish, a new vicar, a new computer and a new manuscript.

David Prior

EDITOR'S PREFACE

'The kingdom of God' said the apostle Paul 'is not talk but power' (1 Cor 4:20). But who would have guessed it, looking at the Church in the West? You could almost reverse Paul's assessment and say that over a good deal of the world 'the kingdom of God is not power but talk'. And a lot of it is talk about matters that are either unreal to most people or of peripheral importance. Look at the agenda of the typical church meeting and you will see what I mean!

Authentic Christianity has always been powerful. Powerful to change the lives of men and women. Powerful to change the attitudes of whole societies. Powerful enough to confront and outlast political system after system. And the source of that power is Jesus of Nazareth. He refuses to be marginalised. Humbly but with enormous authority he challenges the most dearly held prejudices of men and nations. His power was shown in service and in weakness, but the weakness of God is stronger than men.

The theme of Jesus and power is fascinating, and is rarely written about. And this particular book is one I am proud to commend. It will be an enhancement to the Jesus Library. David Prior is a colleague and friend whom I admire. He has had a lot of exposure to power exerted, and power misused, in different countries, not least in the Republic of South Africa where he was a leading clergyman. He is experienced in the 'base communities' of the Latin American world. He has a particular felicity in getting to the heart of the biblical text and making it live. And in these particular studies of Jesus and power we see his work at its best. This is the most significant book David Prior has yet written, and I think you will enjoy it. But I hope you will not leave it there. There is a crying need for Christians not to stay in the religious ghetto but to get out into the places where decisions are made, where the poor are oppressed, where might triumphs over right, and get involved. Jesus did. And it is incumbent upon the Church of Jesus Christ to follow his example. This book will spur us to it.

Michael Green
Professor of Evangelism
Regent College
Vancouver

INTRODUCTION

Power holds a central and all-absorbing place in our daily lives. I never realised the extent of this until I started to study the subject. When I asked my teenage sons to read the newspapers for a week to find illustrations and stories about power, they soon remarked: 'Everything is to do with power.' Even allowing for tunnel vision in the media, the remark emphasised the importance of power in today's world.

In the contemporary world the issue of power, and its use or abuse, is never far from our minds. There is the pervasive question of nuclear power, especially in the wake of the Chernobyl disaster in 1986. The economic power wielded by the West over the rest of the world is high on many agendas (normally for discussion only, not for action). The techno-logical explosion of the last forty or so years has placed immense power in the hands of the communicators and the possessors of massive information banks. The power of tele-vision, with or without the influence of advertising, has completely changed millions of lives. The power of money, highlighted by recent publicity about practices in the City of London and the impact of the 'Big Bang', has become a major political issue. At the more personal level the power of sex is frequently abused, resulting in the destruction of individuals, families and even the fabric of society itself. The AIDS menace highlights this particular abuse of one kind of personal power.

In the life of the Christian church issues of power also predominate. For example, the power of the institutional church, both in its ecclesiastical structures and in its sluggish response to change, leaves most Christians in a confusion of screaming frustration and sad resignation. Where spiritual life flows, the life can so easily be sapped by preoccupation with side issues or by the domination of strong personalities. The power exercised by gifted speakers or popular teachers often seems to go over the top, leaving behind a residue of flatness and disillusionment. There are also Christians who, with the media egging them on, pronounce in public on moral issues, with the focus not on Christ and his gospel but on the need to uphold moral standards – the result being that ordinary people hear the power of moral condemnation rather than the power of God for salvation. Recently Christians were not willing to join in a city-wide mission unless 'power evangelism' of a certain kind was central to every meeting. We have not moved that far from the once familiar situation where certain people had the power to write off others as 'unsound' without giving them an opportunity to explain their stance and their goals.

But of course these issues of power are not only true of today. The Roman historian Tacitus once remarked: 'The lust for power, for dominating others, influences the heart more than any other passion.'[1] The German philosopher Friedrich Nietzsche observed: 'Wherever I found a living creature, I found the unconditioned will to power, to overpower.'[2] Bertrand Russell agreed: 'Of the infinite desires of man, the chief are the desires for power and for glory.'[3]

Even in the most public and obvious arenas of power there is much that is delusive. The American economist J. K. Galbraith, who has been as close as any to the corridors of power in Washington, once remarked: 'Much of what is called power is, in practice, the illusion of power.'[4] Many who have traversed these corridors testify more to their sense of impotence and frustration than to any sense of fulfilment or ability to bring change. Not a few powerful individuals have expressed public relief when they have been relieved of such positions of influence. Indira Gandhi was one such person: once called the most powerful woman in the world, she was glad to be ousted and said so – but she was back as prime minister of India within four years.

There seems, therefore, to be an inherent pull to power. John F. Kennedy admitted it: 'I run for President because that is where the action is.'[5] Perhaps William Hazlitt hit the nail on the head when he observed: 'The love of power is the love of ourselves.'[6] This truth was expanded by Bertrand de Jouvenal: 'Command is a mountain-top. The air breathed there is different, and the perspectives seen there are different, from those of the valley of obedience.'[7]

This evocative phrase 'the valley of obedience' is an apposite introduction to the theme of Jesus and power. At every turn and in every detail Jesus revealed an utterly different kind of power. Because the theme of power is so central to everyday human experience, to study Jesus and power is to study the everyday life of Jesus – and the way he both treated power of a worldly kind and exercised power of a non-worldly kind.

It is a theme of fundamental importance for the Christian church set in the global village of the last fifteen years of the twentieth century. Paul Tournier gives us some explicit reasons:

> Ever since the Renaissance, the flames of human ambition and covetousness (or thirst for power) have been fanned. The sickness is our headlong dash for power. Power has become the supreme value, the only one that is universally recognised – all kinds of power: military, political, economic, industrial; the power of propaganda, publicity and fashion; the power of technology, of organisation of standardisation, of the concentration of big business and its trusts; the power of the masses, of sexual desires; the power of youth, of muscular strength and records counted in hundredths of a second; the power of money and of wealth . . .[8]

Equally penetrating is the opposite side of the same coin. Tournier continues, 'The glorification of the powerful has gone along with the devaluation of the weak, the old, the sensitive, the shy, the scrupulous, the odd, the abandoned and the dreamers.'[9] If it is correct, Tournier's analysis shows how urgent is the need for Christians to re-examine Jesus' attitude towards and use of power. We have almost certainly become so moulded by the world around us that we cannot see how far we have moved from the way of Jesus.

Tournier's examples, both of the powerful and the powerless, cover a wide spectrum of arenas in which the theme of
Jesus and power needs to be applied. In the last three or four
years some excellent books have been published which take a
thorough look at specific areas in which Christians should be
operating in line with the teaching and model of Jesus. I think,
for example, of those by Richard Foster, John Perkins, Jim
Wallis, Jacques Ellul, Henri Nouwen, Cheryl Forbes, Tony
Campolo – all of which I have enjoyed and have mentioned in
the bibliography.

Because these – and other – authors have already done so
with clarity and authority, I have deliberately chosen not to
pursue some of the major contemporary issues at length or
depth. Instead, I have decided to concentrate on the actual
text of the New Testament (mainly the four gospels) and to
draw out key principles to do with Jesus and power.

Strangely enough, most of the authors I have mentioned
have not attempted this with any thoroughness – either
because they were making generalisations from the overall
impact of Jesus' life, or because they reckoned (presumably)
that such ordinary spadework had already been done by
others and that its results were readily accessible. I found
neither assumption to be necessarily true. Obviously there
are major academic studies on very specific aspects of power
as it impinged on and was demonstrated by Jesus. But I could
not run down any more general, but overarching, examination of Jesus' whole life as it relates to the theme of power.

In fact some of the most detailed analysis has been done by
Latin American writers, most of whom would be regarded as
'liberation theologians'. I have studied a dozen or so of their
contributions and sometimes quote from their writings. I have
also been honed in my overall thinking by seven years or more
in South Africa. Over the years, through both their writing
and their talking, men like David Bosch, Desmond Tutu,
Michael Cassidy and John de Gruchy have been immensely
influential in crystallising for me the essence of biblical Christianity in a revolutionary setting. Perhaps the single most
helpful book for background reading also comes from South
Africa – Albert Nolan's *Jesus Before Christianity*.[10]

*   *   *

Jesus and Power is a small attempt to help Christians recover and apply in our behaviour and attitudes Jesus' priorities concerning all aspects of power.

The traditional way into the subject is to begin with a distinction between two New Testament Greek words that are generally translated 'power' and 'authority' – *dunamis* and *exousia* respectively. The first word refers to the actual energy or strength released; the second word refers to an inherent or authorised capacity to be in charge. Among ordinary men and women in the world, it is usually explained, there is a lot of *dunamis*, but without *exousia*. The point about Jesus was that his *dunamis* was a consistent expression of his *exousia*, which he received from God.

Actually, I have never found such semantic analysis particularly helpful or illuminating; doubtless I am not alone in that experience. By contrast, the more I became involved in studying the way Jesus lived his life in the different power situations of his day, the more I began to appreciate how radically I needed to be changed. Maybe the *dunamis/exousia* distinction was intended to bring me to the same place; but it never did so. Perhaps the word games obscured the sheer immensity of the contrast Jesus had introduced between human power and God's power. Whatever the case, you will not find such verbal distinctions in this book. I have tried instead to get inside the heartbeat of Jesus' ministry and mission. As I have made this attempt, I have found myself inevitably drawn into an investigation of his whole identity and person. I have not ventured into the Old Testament. It might seem, superficially at least, that parts of the Old Testament tell a rather different story from that of Jesus and power. I doubt whether this is true. To quote one comment on the phrase 'the righteous', one of several terms in the Old Testament for God's people:

It presents them as those who honour God and order their lives in all things according to his will. In every human relationship they faithfully fulfil the obligations that the relationship entails, remembering that power and authority (of whatever sort: domestic, social, political, economic, religious, intellectual) are to be used to bless, not to exploit (John Stek).[11]

I am, finally, not unaware of the theological minefields into which I am trespassing, especially in the no-(lay)man's-land of Christology. I have attempted to read around this particular subject, within the considerable limits of my personal schedule and resources. I trust that any theological blunders will not be so heinous as to invalidate the overall impact of the book. The impact will not be that of new truth, only that of the truth, as it is in Jesus, applied to our lives. As Pascal once said: 'All the good maxims have been written. It only remains to put them into practice.'[12]

1 WEAK AND HELPLESS – THE POWER OF A BABY

A baby has an unique capacity to attract attention and to become the most important person in the room. A baby provides a talking point and breaks down many barriers – barriers of shyness, sadness, strangeness, even of complete non-communication between people of different nationalities and languages who cannot otherwise relate to each other.

At the same time, a baby is completely helpless, vulnerable, dependent; it is powerless to do anything for itself except feed, scream, burp and sleep – and most of these require some assistance. A baby is powerful in its powerlessness. So it was with Jesus, the baby son of Mary. In spite of his identity (Emmanuel, 'God with us', Matt 1:23), the significance of his name (Jesus, 'for he will save his people from their sins', Matt 1:21) and his destiny ('a ruler who will govern my people Israel', Matt 2:6), this baby was as powerless then as he became later, when hanging high on the Roman cross of execution as a young man in his early thirties.

As Matthew and Luke both intend us to understand, this baby exercised immense power in his powerlessness – power to attract the attention of those who wanted to worship him and those who wanted to eliminate him. Baby-worshippers are legion; baby-killers are, mercifully, rare. Further consideration will explain more clearly what made some people worshippers and others enemies.

Matthew 2 provides the bulk of our information.[1] We are told that 'when Jesus was born in Bethlehem of Judea in the days of Herod the king, behold, wise men from the East came to Jerusalem, saying, "Where is he who has been born king of the Jews?"' (Matt 2:1–2). These few words open up a fascinating perspective on the Jewish world at the time of Jesus.

The expectation of a Messiah, promised for centuries in the Old Testament scriptures, was neither forgotten nor prominent among the Jews. It was in place, but lengthening years of foreign occupation had eroded its cutting edge.[2] From time to time possible deliverers emerged, but they were soon extinguished.[3]

On the other hand, 'There is abundant evidence of a wide-spread desire and expectation of a coming Deliverer or universal King some time before the Birth of Christ.'[4] The most vivid, relevant and well-known expression of this expectation is found in the Roman poet Virgil, who in his fourth Eclogue, written in 40 BC, describes the birth of a special child who will usher in a 'glorious age' in which 'he will rule over a world made peaceful by the virtues of his father'. The poem talks of endless fruitfulness in the earth, the destruction of baneful influences, and the end of warfare. 'Let such times come soon' is the plea of the poet.[5]

Wise men from the East

Into this tired but yearning world Jesus was born to be king. Matthew's account of the long journey undertaken by 'wise men from the East' is intended to reflect this human search, as well as to throw into sharp relief the vicious hostility of King Herod. If we include also the part played by the chief priests and the scribes on the one hand, and the shepherds out in their fields on the other (as recorded by Luke), we have a fourfold perspective on the impact caused by this newborn baby: wise men from the East, Herod the king, chief priests, shepherds. To each came a revelation from God – by means of a star, through private information, via the Old Testament scriptures, and from an angel of the Lord. The evangelists want us to notice what each did with God's revelation concerning his Son.

The wise men were 'magi' – a term used loosely to cover 'a wide variety of men interested in dreams, astrology, magic, books thought to contain mysterious references to the future, and the like. Some Magi honestly inquired after truth; many were rogues and charlatans . . .'[6] The studies of these particular magi had led them to expect a new king in Judea. By means of an exceptional star, they were led to Jerusalem – with one intention: 'We . . . have come to worship him' (Matt 2:2). When they eventually found 'the child with Mary his mother' (Matt 2:11), they fell down and worshipped him, offering the most valuable gifts they had with them. The story is quite remarkable and Matthew's purpose in recounting it is clear:

> Pagans, who had nothing to guide them but smatterings of science mingled with much superstition, nevertheless are so kindled with enthusiasm by the signs which God, by means of these imperfect instruments, had granted to them, that they take a long journey and make careful investigation, in order to pay due reverence to the new Ruler who has been sent into the world.[7]

Herod the king

Herod, by contrast, wanted Jesus eliminated. That was in character. Born in 73 BC, Herod the Great (as he came to be known) was named king of the Roman-occupied province of Judea by the Roman senate in 40 BC. Within a few years he had crushed all opposition to his rule and proceeded to run the province, hand-in-glove with the occupying legions, with extreme skill and success. He was wealthy, politically gifted, an excellent administrator and clever enough to remain in the good graces of successive Roman emperors. He was well known both for his impressive building projects (including the temple at Jerusalem) and for the exorbitant taxes he levied from the people to finance them all. His brilliance was seen especially in the way he tackled famine relief – a national disaster which even the massive administrative machinery of the twentieth century cannot solve.

Herod loved power and would resort to anything to retain and – as he thought – secure it more firmly. He was incredibly cruel, suspicious and resentful – cruel in completely callous disregard for human life; suspicious of any conceivable rival, pretender or even successor to his throne; and sullen in his resentment towards the Jewish people, who regarded him as a usurper of the throne from which he ruled so arrogantly and viciously.

Matthew would have us take note of this in his juxtaposition of 'he who has been born king of the Jews' and 'Herod the king' (Matt 2:2, 3). Jesus was born king of the Jews, Herod had been put there at the age of thirty-three by an alien government. At the age of thirty-three, or thereabouts, Jesus was to secure his kingship on a Roman cross of execution outside the city walls of Herod's Jerusalem. One of the fascinating little details of Matthew's gospel is that the title 'king of the Jews', first pronounced by these eastern magi, is found again only in the title inscribed on that Roman cross at the end of this baby's short life.

Herod's violent actions have been documented in some detail by the Jewish historian Josephus, whose accounts are not always to be trusted. It seems, however, that in his later years Herod suffered an illness which compounded his paranoia, and that he turned to unpredictable acts of unrestrained cruelty.

In 7 BC – presumably only a short time before the birth of Jesus – he had two of his sons by Mariamne, Alexander and Aristobulus, put to death because he feared their rivalry for his throne. They had been educated at Rome and were known to the then Caesar, Augustus, who is reputed to have reacted: 'It is better to be Herod's pig than his son.' It seems that Herod dispatched another of his sons, Antipater, in 4 BC; had his wife and several close associates murdered; arranged to have hundreds of Jewish leaders executed on the day of his death (to 'safeguard' his son Archelaus in his reign); and so inspired Archelaus that he inaugurated his own reign with a massacre of three thousand people – again, we presume, because they threatened his position. Against the backcloth of this rampant violence, the murder of probably a dozen or so Bethlehem boys under two years old, in an attempt to eliminate Jesus, assumes rather morbidly reduced proportions. It was a mild atrocity by comparison with Herod's career of cruelty.

We can easily relegate this catalogue of crimes to the 'primitive' days of two thousand years ago – until we pause to recollect the events of the last sixty or seventy years in Stalin's

Russia (and ever since), Hitler's Germany, many Latin American countries, and actions of the Khmer Rouge in Cambodia, or the mass killings in Amin's (and Obote's) Uganda, Gaddafi's Libya, Khomeini's Iran and Bokassa's Central African Republic.

The story of Herod the Great is the story of the twentieth century as much as of two thousand years ago. It is the story of any ruler who loves power and finds the presence, or even the rumoured proximity, of any other king intolerable in its menace to the status quo. When Matthew refers precisely to Herod 'the king', he is explaining why 'he was troubled' (Matt 2:3): his throne was in danger. And when he records that this turmoil affected 'all Jerusalem with him' (Matt 2:3), he is not exaggerating. The people of that violent city knew all too well that if Herod was troubled they could expect widespread reprisals to be carried out ruthlessly and indiscriminately. This was the impact of a baby on the nation's king.

The chief priests

If Herod was resented as a puppet ruler, a usurper and a betrayer of true Judaism through his allegiance to the Romans, the chief priests and the scribes represented 'pukka' national purity, pride and propriety. They knew the Old Testament scriptures backwards: that was their job. They knew all about national expectations of a Messiah. Within their own lifetime they had probably had to deal with both popular enquiries and potential claimants to the title. When summoned by Herod, with whom they had only smouldering, distant and rare contact, they could immediately give the right biblical answers to his questions about 'the Christ'.

Matthew unambiguously contrasts the enthusiastic and costly adoration of the magi, who had so little and such muddled information to go on, with the sheer apathy of the religious leaders, who had the extensive light of both the law and the prophets to illuminate them. If there was a possibility that the Christ had been born, implies Matthew, should they not have been up and doing? If pagan visitors could travel hundreds, if not thousands, of miles to worship the king,

could they not jerk themselves into a short ten-mile trip to
Bethlehem? Calvin, with characteristic pungency, refers to
their 'base sluggishness'.[8] It was not every day, let alone
night, that Eastern magi arrived in Jerusalem; and it was
certainly not every day that Herod asked for their help. Yet
the chief priests did not interrupt their regular routine: it was
too inconvenient.

It was to such 'blind leaders of the blind' that Jesus was later
to declare: 'You search the scriptures, because you think that
in them you have eternal life; and it is they that bear witness to
me; yet you refuse to come to me that you may have life'
(John 5:39–40). That refusal to travel a few miles to come to
the baby Jesus was prophetic of the personal journey which
the religious leaders refused to make in order to come to the
man Jesus thirty years later. Unchecked apathy still culmi-
nates in outright rejection. How many men and women who
are today in positions of power, including religious power,
failed in earlier years – when they were so close (perhaps at a
Christmas carol service or in Sunday school or at a youth
camp or mission) – through sheer apathy or 'base sluggishness' to make the journey to Bethlehem to worship the King?
Now the journey is long and costly, too costly: 'you refuse to
come to me'.

Shepherds in the fields

Luke provides us with the account of 'shepherds out in the
field, keeping watch over their flock by night' (Luke 2:8).
Unlike the magi, the chief priests and scribes, and Herod the
king, the shepherds were unexceptional, ordinary folk, mind-
ing their own cold and unglamorous business in the fields
outside Bethlehem. They reflect Luke's emphasis, noticeable
throughout his gospel, on ordinary people. But we also need
to appreciate that shepherding was not a very respectable
occupation in those days in that country. 'Shepherds were
considered untrustworthy' – they often pastured their flocks
on fields belonging to others. In addition, 'their work made
them ceremonially unclean'.[9] In other words shepherds were
social outcasts. Luke retains this focus throughout his account

of Jesus' public ministry: the rejects and despised among his contemporaries were the ones who were drawn to him and responded with joy to his message.

The shepherds, therefore, are 'forerunners . . . of future believers who will glorify God for what they have heard and will praise God for what they have seen'.[10] They also 'symbolize all the ordinary people who have joyfully received the gospel and have become in various ways pastors to others'.[11] It was – and is – to such ordinary people that God afforded the full splendour of revelation by an angel and through a multitude of heavenly hosts bent on praise. It would have been difficult *not* to go looking for the baby under such circumstances. The shepherds were under no illusions, the Lord himself had made known to them the remarkable events in Bethlehem. They acted on the revelation 'with haste' (Luke 2:16). They also did not refrain from making known to anyone who would listen everything that the angel had told them about the baby in the manger.

Distant foreigners showing their wisdom by diligently looking for the baby; a frightened ruler seeking to get rid of the baby; experts with their heads crammed with the right facts but apathetic about the baby; ignored and rejected peasants responding with alacrity to angelic revelation about the baby – these four underline the power of the powerless baby. Why? Because he was who he was: Emmanuel, 'God with us'.

In the incarnation of the Son of God, the purposes and the very person of God became enfleshed. The whole created universe was now engaged in encounter with its creator: stars, kings, shepherds, priests, angels; rich and poor; near and far; powerful and impotent. Never had God been more vulnerable; never had God been so powerful. A life had begun – one lasting only a little over thirty years – which in its sheer divestiture of power was to exercise immeasurable and irresistible power over all people and all creation.

Matthew explains, indirectly but unmistakably, in his second chapter how the reality of Emmanuel, 'God with us', involved Jesus both in fragile vulnerability and in eternal security. He stresses this by way of sovereign intervention into the parental care exercised by Joseph and by emphasising the fulfilment of Old Testament scriptures. Herod's fury, the

Egyptian exile, the uncertainty of Archelaus' disposition: none of these precarious situations could thwart the purposes of God for and in Jesus.

Nevertheless, we should not so highlight the controlling protection of God almighty that we fail to appreciate the pervasive powerlessness of 'God with us' in Jesus. Every last detail of the infancy narratives in both Matthew and Luke brings this overriding truth into sharp focus. God decided to strip himself of anything which might insulate him from naked encounter and identification with the world and the people he had created.

It has been traditional to see this self-humbling as God in some way hiding or suspending or adding to or relinquishing his divinity in order to become man. But what if he was, in Jesus, actually *uncovering* his divinity? Does the baby of Bethlehem not reveal God rather than obscure him? Is God's nature not seen in the powerlessness (to human estimation) of the baby?

Jesus and children

This would remain relatively distant and, at best, suggestive rather than central for Christian discipleship, were it not for specific events and teaching in the later life of this baby, Jesus. In Matthew's gospel there are three incidents towards the end of his public ministry which have direct and eloquent bearing on our theme of Jesus and power. In each one the presence of children, very young children, babies, is paramount. In all three incidents Matthew uses the same word as is used seven times of the baby Jesus in Matthew 2. Although this word, *teknion*, cannot be applied exclusively to infants, it is used in this way so consistently that we need not doubt that babes-in-arms or extremely young children were at the centre of the stage.

The first occasion (Matt 18:1–14) concerns a question which rarely seemed to be far from the conversations held by the twelve disciples: 'Who is the greatest in the kingdom of heaven?' In both Matthew and Luke the discussion appears to follow almost immediately on yet another statement from

Jesus about his imminent death (Matt 17:22–23; Luke 9:43–45). In response to their questions, Jesus placed a little child in their midst – in fact Mark says that he took the child in his arms, thus reinforcing the very young age of the child (Mark 9:36). First Jesus uses the child to teach how we *enter* the kingdom of heaven; then he stresses the need for us to humble ourselves 'like this child', if we are to be the greatest in the kingdom. In all three synoptic gospels Jesus declares finally that 'Whoever receives one such child in my name receives me' (Matt 18:5; cf. Mark 9:37; Luke 9:48).

A baby becomes, therefore, an illustration of three cardinal truths about the kingdom of God: how we enter, how we find true greatness, and how we welcome Jesus himself into our midst. A helpless dependent baby provides the clue for all three profound truths. What did Jesus mean?

The challenge to the disciples is, first of all, to turn and become like children, like babies:

> . . . the meaning seems to be that by raising this question of precedence the disciples had gone in the wrong direction. They evidently did not know where true greatness was to be found; and, if they desire to enter the Kingdom, they must remember the first Beatitude and return to the childlike attitude, which does not seek prominence but shrinks from it.[12]

For modern, as well as the original, disciples such conversion is difficult and humbling. It involves throwing ourselves in complete dependence on the mercy and power of God as our Father, acknowledging that we have no innate power to help ourselves and no merit to recommend us to God. When we become like little children in this sense, totally vulnerable before God and our fellows, we find that the kingdom of heaven is ours.

True childlikeness

It is not merely a question of entering the kingdom of God, but of experiencing the continuous rule of God. That requires

consistently humbling ourselves like a little child. A baby
does not suddenly decide to launch out on its own, independently of its parents; it remains dependent and unconcerned
for anything except its parents' love and provision. We never
grow out of being little children in this sense. For example,
Paul exhorts infantile Christians at Corinth to grow up out of
their constant bickering (1 Cor 3:1–4) – strangely enough, this
was quite akin to the disciples' arguments around Jesus: at
Corinth they were always arguing about who was the greatest
preacher/teacher/minister of the gospel. Paul urged them to
leave such petty squabbling completely behind, because he
wanted them to grow up into mature manhood (cf. 1 Cor
14:20; Eph 4:14). The Corinthians were fairly infantile in
their thinking at the best of times: the rivalry was just one
more example. They had, like the first disciples of Jesus,
forgotten the *true* childlikeness of resting in the unequivocal
and uncompromising love of their Father, from whom they
had received everything they now enjoyed (1 Cor 4:7). They
needed to humble themselves to discover the true greatness of
complete dependence on God. We can visualise the baby
resting peacefully in the arms of Jesus as he said these words.

Jesus takes the teaching one stage further by declaring that
he comes to us in a little child: 'Whoever receives one such
child in my name receives me' (Matt 18:5). The very vulnerability and dependence of a baby, created in the image of
God, acts as an incarnation of Jesus, who finds himself at
home in a little child – and at home, also, in the hearts of those
who make room and time for little children. A baby is the
ideal medium of self-revelation for the Son of God, because in
a baby he can most readily display what God is like. We know
this only because of his own birth as a baby at Bethlehem; but,
knowing it, we do well to make this truth our own by the way
we welcome little children. In many societies and, more sadly,
in many churches the children are regarded as a nuisance – a
disruption that is of secondary importance and better kept
apart from adults.

Jesus tackled this attitude to little children head-on in the
second incident described by Matthew (Matt 19:13–15):
'Then children were brought to [Jesus] that he might lay his
hands on them and pray. The disciples rebuked the people;

but Jesus said, "Let the children come to me, and do not hinder them; for to such belongs the kingdom of heaven."'
The first point to notice is how soon this incident occurs after the one we have just examined. Disciples of Jesus learn slowly. The teaching about being humble like a little child had clearly gone in one ear and out the other. It is very difficult to humble ourselves to the point where we jettison the worldly notions of greatness and importance with which we are brought up.

The necessity of continuing in a childlike openness to God is underlined by the way in which Jesus, at a cardinal moment in his ministry, adamantly affirms that only such childlike people can receive God's revelation of his truth and power. In Luke's account Jesus is 'debriefing' the seventy disciples on their return from a successful mission. They had seen remarkable demonstrations of God's sovereign power over all the forces of evil. After urging them not to concentrate on these wonderful experiences but on the security of their salvation from God, Jesus 'in that same hour . . . rejoiced in the Holy Spirit and said, "I thank thee, Father, Lord of heaven and earth, that thou hast hidden these things from the wise and understanding and revealed them to babes; yea, Father, for such was thy gracious will"' (Luke 10:21). Here was a large group of disciples being childlike with open trust in the commission and promises of Jesus – to these disciples God could reveal what not only wise and understanding men of the world but even 'prophets and kings desired to see . . . and to hear' (Luke 10:24).

In Matthew's account of a similar situation – if not the same one – Jesus is again recorded as thanking his Father in prayer for revealing the secrets of his kingly rule to 'babes', while keeping them hidden from 'the wise and understanding' (Matt 11:25). The immediate context in Matthew, however, is not the mission of the seventy, but the open invitation to all weary and heavy-laden people to find rest in him. Although that particular invitation is not found in Luke, its substance was at the heart of the gospel of the kingdom entrusted to the seventy. The key truth in both Matthew and Luke is Jesus' insistence on the childlike, babylike character of true discipleship. We do not grow as disciples unless God chooses to reveal to us more and more of himself. Any tendency to pride and self-dependence blocks this revelation and therefore halts growth.

This becomes glaringly apparent when we turn to Matthew's third account of little children in prominence around Jesus, this time on Palm Sunday (Matt 21:12–17). He has ridden into Jerusalem on a donkey, driven the profiteers out of the temple, and begun to heal the blind and the lame who came to him in the temple. In the face of such 'wonderful things' one might have expected men of religion to recognise the presence and power of God. As we know, the very opposite proved true: 'But when the chief priests and the scribes saw [what he did] . . . they were indignant . . .' They were incensed by virtually everything happening around them; but the last straw came when the little children started to cry out in the temple, 'Hosanna to the Son of David!' This uncomplicated testimony to Jesus as Messiah – the result of divine revelation to children, but the depth of blasphemy to blind and proud priests – proved to be the catalyst for another powerful endorsement of childlikeness by Jesus: 'have you never read, "Out of the mouth of babes and sucklings thou has brought perfect praise"?'

To be a disciple of Jesus and a child of the kingdom is to live dangerously; it means that we are vulnerable to the scepticism and hostility of those who rely for power on wisdom, under-standing, knowledge or status. However fierce or cynical this opposition might become, we have the assurance of Jesus that such 'little ones' are infinitely precious to God (Matt 18:5–9). Jesus plainly issues dire warnings to anyone who disturbs the childlike faith of any disciple. He also vividly describes the immense love of the good shepherd for even one lost sheep, as a picture of the heavenly Father's protective love of each of his children (Matt 18:10–14). Childlike disciples may be 'little ones', 'babes', 'little children' and therefore be exposed to many perils of a similar kind to the baby Jesus. But, also like that baby, our very vulnerability serves to mirror the character of God.

Power in helplessness

Perhaps, therefore, the power of God is seen consummately in the helplessness of a baby, as a paradigm and a precursor of the helplessness of a crucified man. If this proves to be the case, our notions – not just of power but of God himself – may need to be radically revised. We might then be nearer to understanding the paradox expressed by Paul, 'when I am weak, then I am strong' (2 Cor 12:10).

In his book *Gracias*, Henri Nouwen illustrates this with the following comments on the birth of Laura, the Down's syndrome baby of his brother and sister-in-law.

> Laura is going to be important for all of us in the family. We have never had a 'weak' person among us. We are all hardworking, ambitious and successful people who seldom have to experience powerlessness. Now Laura enters and tells us a totally new story, a story of weakness, brokenness, vulnerability and total dependency. Laura, who will always be a child, will teach us the way of Christ as no-one will ever be able to do.[13]

Was this also what Paul was trying to express in the famous hymn of Christ's glory in Philippians 2? Yes, Jesus was 'in the form of God'; he knew what it was to be equal with God; but he was 'born in the likeness of men' in order to show us the essential nature of God. God is like that; God's nature is to humble himself, not to assert himself; God's nature is as a servant, not as an overlord; he wins by submitting, by serving, by stooping, by pouring himself out, by emptying himself.

In his thorough and illuminating book *New Testament Theology*, Donald Guthrie clearly favours this possible rendering of the text. The original would then be translated: 'Christ Jesus regarded equality with God in terms of no-snatching' – i.e. as being expressed in giving rather than gaining. He comments: 'There is much to be said for [this interpretation], for it would fit the context better if Christ's action could more readily serve as a pattern for man's action.' Such an interpretation would involve a rendering of the theological time bomb 'emptied himself' more along the lines of 'he poured himself out' – i.e. understood as 'self-effacement, the antithesis of the self-aggrandizement which would follow if Jesus had snatched at the glory which was later to be bestowed upon him'.[14]

We have this 'mind' available to us in Christ Jesus. That true power is for us, if we will exchange our human – very human – notions of power for his. In a word, it is the power of love, love which lays down our lives as he laid down his life. We are most like God when we lay down our lives, when we walk the road he trod in line with his own words: 'If any man would come after me, let him deny himself and take up his cross daily and follow me' (Luke 9:23). We reflect the character and nature of God most accurately when we thus lay down our lives.

The options in front of us

Like the magi from the East, we can come to worship such a king; or, like Herod, we can seek to eliminate such a rule of powerful love from our lives. We can carry on as before, like the religious leaders, not bothering to let such a king disturb our comfortable routine; or we can join the shepherds in joyfully proclaiming what we have come to see and in praising God for his revolutionary self-disclosure in a baby.

This, then, is the likely meaning of the prophecies surrounding the birth of this baby: 'From you [Bethlehem] shall come a ruler who will govern my people Israel . . .' (Matt 2:6; cf. Mic 5:2); 'He will be great and will be called the Son of the Most High; and the Lord God will give to him the throne of his father David, and he will reign over the house of Jacob for ever; and of his kingdom there will be no end' (Luke 1:32–33). When the apostles bore witness to 'the power of his resurrection' (see, e.g., Phil 3:10; cf. 2 Cor 12:9; Eph 1:19) and 'the power of the Holy Spirit' (cf. Acts 1:8; Rom 15:13; Eph 3:16; 2 Tim 1:7), they were surely referring to the power of God to write such a kingly rule into the hearts and lives of his people. The kingdom of God comes when men and women allow God's Spirit to give them *this* new life, which is to be found only in Jesus. In the prologue to his gospel, John puts the same truth in his own distinctive way:

The true light that enlightens every man was coming into the world. He was in the world, and the world was made through him, yet the world knew him not. He came to his own home, and his own people received him not. But to all who received him, who believed in his name, he gave power to become children of God. (John 1:9–12)

We can see, therefore, that the power of the risen Lord Jesus, poured out to us from on high in the gift of his Spirit, is not in essence a power to rival or outstrip human power: it is the power to be like Jesus, who has shown us the true nature of God. It is the power to be a servant, to humble ourselves, to be (in human terms) powerless. It is the power to live – and to die – for others. It is the power to resist the temptations to exercise power in purely human, worldly or even satanic ways. This particular aspect of our theme is the subject of our next chapter: the temptations of Jesus in the wilderness.

Listen to Henri Nouwen again:

Somehow I keep expecting loud and impressive events to convince me and others of God's saving power; but over and over again I am reminded that spectacles, power-plays and big events are the ways of the world. Our temptation is to be distracted by them. When I have no eyes for the sweet signs of God's presence – the smile of a baby, the carefree play of children, the words of encouragement and gestures of love offered by friends – I will always remain tempted to despair. The small child of Bethlehem, the unknown young man of Nazareth, the rejected preacher, the naked man on the cross, *he* asks for my full attention. The work of our salvation takes place in the midst of a world that continues to shout, scream and overwhelm us with its claims and promises.[15]

2 TAKING THE EASY WAY – POWER STRUGGLE

Power is a fact of life. We all exercise a measure of power: husbands over wives and wives over husbands; parents over children and children over parents; management over employees and employees over management; government over people and (sometimes and in some places) people over government; church leaders over church members and church members over church leaders. The debate and the problems are not concerned with the existence or even with the achievement of power so much as with its exercise. How is the power we possess to be used?

This was the crucial and determinative issue for Jesus at the outset of his public ministry. The evangelists, with their subtle nuances of emphasis, all make the same point: 'Then Jesus was led up by the Spirit into the wilderness to be tempted by the devil' (Matt 4:1); 'The Spirit immediately drove him out into the wilderness. And he was in the wilderness forty days, tempted by Satan' (Mark 1:12–13); 'And Jesus, full of the Holy Spirit, returned from the Jordan, and was led by the Spirit for forty days in the wilderness, tempted by the devil' (Luke 4:1–2).

The temptations follow his baptism in the Jordan by John, when God has borne witness to him with the Spirit descending like a dove and alighting on him, together with a clear word of attestation: 'This is my beloved Son, with whom I am well pleased' (Matt 3:17; cf. Mark 1:11; Luke 3:22). So Jesus has been well and truly launched on his mission as God's Son, as the Messiah. He is 'full of the Holy Spirit', responding to the thrusting power of the Spirit as he moves to meet the testings of Satan. He knows the power and presence of God in his life: but what will he do with it? How will he make use of that power? 'It was in God's plan that . . . Jesus should face up to the question of what kind of Messiah He was to be.'[1]

Popular expectations

We need to remember that the Jewish people were looking for a saviour and a liberator from the occupation forces of Rome. They wanted and expected this Messiah to exercise power in a particular manner, i.e. as a conquering king, with the strength of arms if necessary. These popular expectations continued to be essential ingredients of Satan's temptations to Jesus throughout his public ministry.

Jesus had God's work to do. He had God's power at his disposal for the task. Satan's temptations represented 'an attempt to overthrow the Messiah at the very opening of His public career as the Saviour of the world'.[2]

When we pause to recollect that the details of the temptations could have come only from Jesus himself, presumably in later private sessions with his disciples, we can appreciate how important it is to get inside the temptations: they provide a unique insight into the inner pressures which faced him, and will always face his disciples.

When Luke places the temptations of Jesus immediately after his genealogy back to 'Adam, the son of God' (Luke 3:38), instead of directly after his baptism, he is presumably wanting us to see the contrast between Adam 'who though tested in the bliss of Eden yet fell, and Jesus, who was tested in the hardships of the wilderness yet triumphed'.[3] The essence of this power struggle is fundamental to the human experience. Adam had God's work to do and God's presence and power to do it, but he failed. What would happen to 'the second Adam'?

Another parallel or contrast is presented by Matthew and Luke in the way their narratives make steady use of the book of Deuteronomy; in fact all the quotations come from Deuteronomy 6–8, which comments on Israel's experiences in the wilderness through forty long years. Israel, God's 'son', failed to meet the test; Jesus, God's Son, now moves to face similar testing through these forty days in the wilderness. 'The temptations were . . . a re-enactment of the temptations of Israel. Jesus is seen as the exemplar of the new Israel and his disciples are expected to imitate him.'[4] It is the character and the destiny of God's people that are at stake. In this power struggle, it can readily be seen, the stakes are very high.

In these ways Jesus came to 'destroy [or 'unravel'] the works of the devil' (1 John 3:8). He was propelled by the Spirit into this fierce time of testing because there would be no salvation for Israel or for mankind without victory in this arena. Essential to the victory was the way the victory was achieved. This will become plain as we look at each temptation in turn.

Stones into bread

The temptation to turn stones into bread and the temptation to hurl himself off the pinnacle of the temple are both frequently interpreted primarily as attempts by Satan to make Jesus doubt his identity as the Son of God: 'If you are the Son of God . . .' (Matt 4:3, 6; Luke 4:3, 9). 'There may be a hint of that in Satan's words; but it is more likely that Satan was not inviting Jesus to doubt his sonship but to reflect on its meaning'.[5] If he is the Son of God, this surely means he possesses both the power and the right to satisfy his own needs – in this case, for food. The devil wanted to manipulate Jesus into using the authority of his sonship in a way inconsistent both with the work God had given him to do and with the very character of God. A similar temptation came to Jesus at the very end of his ministry and life, when Jewish onlookers cried out to him on the cross: 'If you are the Son of God, come down from the cross' – a taunt which found a ready echo on the lips of the chief priests, scribes and elders (Matt 27:39 –44), as well as of at least one of the criminals being executed beside Jesus.

If Jesus had used the power at his disposal in the way suggested by Satan, he would have betrayed his Father, his mission and his vocation. He would also thereby have failed to reveal the true nature of God. The temptation was, therefore, essentially an appeal to Jesus to exercise his messiahship in a selfish way, for his own comfort and as a short cut to finishing God's work. It was subtle, and yet not so subtle: 'God fed His people by frequent miracles in the wilderness: may not His Son work one miracle to feed Himself? . . . What will become of the Messiah's work, if He allows Himself to perish for want of food?'[6]

The answer of Jesus is unequivocal: 'Man shall not live by bread alone' (Matt 4:4; Luke 4:4) – quoting what God had spoken to the Israelities in the wilderness, thus emphasising the pre-eminent priority of obedience to God's word. God had spoken to his Son plainly and precisely about the work he had come to do: in that was included his preservation from the immediate pressure of hunger. Jesus 'refuses to work a miracle which God has not willed, in order to effect what God has willed'.[7]

This refusal is more than the resolute rejection of an opportunity to use power wrongly and selfishly. Donald Carson states that 'Satan's aim was to entice Jesus to use powers rightly his but which he had voluntarily abandoned to carry out the Father's mission'.[8] This argument suggests that before his incarnation Jesus (and God the Father) used these 'powers' in a way he rejected while a man on earth. From the gospel narratives, however, it seems clear (the feeding of the five thousand is an example) that Jesus still retained such powers in his public ministry. The crunch came with the devil's temptation to use them in the wrong way, because by so doing he would be failing to reflect the character of God. And we know from Genesis 3 that Satan has always attempted to slander or misrepresent the character of God. God is not self-centred or manipulative in the use of his power; in Jesus equality with God can be seen in not-grasping for himself (Phil 2:6).

But if Satan had persuaded Jesus to use his power in such a way, the character of God would have been devastatingly maligned – indeed, if Jesus was indeed the revelation of the Father and the Son in whom the Father was well-pleased, what kind of God would he have turned out to be?

Using power selfishly

How does this temptation, both in its essential content and in the victory of Jesus over its force, affect the lives of his disciples – today? Primarily, it forces us to re-examine the power we ourselves have and, more particularly, the way we exercise it. As we will see later in this chapter, Satan has usurped power in and over the world. We need, therefore, to determine to what extent our power has been contaminated by his influence. We also need to establish the degree to which we are using it for selfish ends, to make our own lives more comfortable or to avoid some of the long-haul discipline involved in following Jesus.

For example, the scriptures clearly affirm a proper authority for parents over children (in, e.g., Eph 6:1–4). But it is all too easy to slip into a dominating authoritarian approach to our children, which, in essence, is self-indulgent and has one eye on a more comfortable existence. The same truth holds painfully good in the husband–wife relationship: the right kind of mutual submission, expressed in a positive and joyful acceptance of God's pattern for marriage, can easily slip over into demanding our rights, instead of fulfilling our responsibilities. To take each of the family situations a stage further, do we use the proper power and authority entrusted to us by the Lord in a way which genuinely reflects the giving, serving, loving nature of God himself?

The same searching principle can be applied to life in the Christian community of a local church. There is a proper authority under the lordship of Jesus to be exercised within the church. But is the power being exercised by Christian leaders truly of God – i.e. is it, first of all, power which God has truly vested in them? And, if it is of such a kind, is it being exercised in a way which reflects the humble servant-character of God in Christ? It is a very simple and common thing for leadership in God's church to be essentially self-serving, with the emphasis on short cuts to spiritual effectiveness and the actual concern of those in leadership lapsing into one for personal fulfilment, ambition, reputation or comfort.

At this early stage in his ministry, Jesus won the battle with the tempter over such a selfish, dominating use of power. It is significant that he won the victory *before* he chose his disciples, initiating three years of laying down his life for them and thus loving them to the very end. Towards the end of those three years he found it necessary, in the light of their self-centred bickering about who was the greatest among them, to make it absolutely plain that on no account should competitive, dominating or aggressive leadership become entrenched or even tolerated in the Christian community: 'You know that those who are supposed to rule over the Gentiles lord it over them, and their great men exercise authority over them. But it shall not be so among you; but whoever would be great among you must be your servant, and whoever would be first among you must be slave of all.' The reason and the inspiration were to be found in the example of Jesus himself: 'For the Son of man also came not to be served but to serve, and to give his life as a ransom for many' (Mark 10:42–45).

True leadership

Mark's account of this teaching has two nuances which are not found in either Matthew or Luke. The first is contained in the phrase 'those who are supposed to rule over the Gentiles', presumably placing a deliberate question mark over the actual substance and legitimacy (from an eternal perspective) of their leadership. The second nuance is Jesus' firm statement that to be number one entails being 'slave of all', not just of some or of a few. With this he summarily removes any notion of leadership among his disciples which retains the faintest whiff of either status or domination.

The equivalent teaching in John's gospel, where he washes the disciples' feet, makes the message even more devastatingly plain. John uses breathtaking language to build up the awesome humility of Jesus' actions. We need note only the following sentence: 'Jesus, knowing that the Father had given all things into his hands, and that he had come from God and was going to God, rose from supper, laid aside his garments, and girded himself with a towel . . . and began to wash the disciples' feet' (John 13:3–5). We are, unfortunately, so

accustomed to the story that we may fail to appreciate the
staggering truth in those words. This is the Son of God
revealing the character of God in a classically 'no-snatching'
action.

The whole movement of John 13 emphasises that Jesus is
not merely doing what his Father has told him to do but
behaving as the Father behaves. In the same way, the servants
of the Master are to 'do as I have done to you' (John 13:15).
True blessedness comes – both to individuals and to churches
– only as we get down to behaving as we see Jesus behaving
and doing what we know to be the truth about Christian
leadership. In this way we not only become aware of God's
true character but we 'receive' him (John 13:20) – the word
means to welcome him into our midst and to make him feel at
home among us. Dominating and selfish use of authority in
the church encourages the absence of God. When you enter
such a church you can even 'feel' that absence.

Trying to manipulate God

In Matthew's account Satan's second temptation consisted in
luring Jesus into hurling himself off the pinnacle of the temple
(Matt 4:5–6): 'It is, after all, the angels' job to guard and
deliver you from all danger,' he insinuated. On the surface
this was an appeal to a spectacular use of his power as the Son
of God. No doubt there would have been many people
around to see such a performance: Jesus, however, pinpointed the essence of this temptation in his unequivocal
answer from the scriptures – 'You shall not tempt the Lord
your God.' However important it is to notice the readiness
with which Satan quoted the Old Testament, it is far more
important to appreciate the nub of the tempter's assault: he
was attempting to make the Son of God use his sonship to
force God into action on his behalf. This is not trust and
obedience, but holding a gun to God's head in an attempt to
manipulate him into doing what we want – instead of being
available to him to do what he wants.

Calvin has some incisive remarks on this temptation:
'in this passage, the word *tempt* denotes the neglect of

those means which he [God] puts into our hands'.[9] As with the Israelites in the wilderness, Jesus was being tempted to demand miraculous protection as proof of God's care. The narrative in Exodus is clear: 'And he [Moses] called the name of the place Massah [that is 'Proof'] and Meribah [that is 'Contention'], because of the faultfinding of the children of Israel, and because they put the Lord to the proof by saying, "Is the Lord among us or not?"' (Exod 17:7). Tempting God, or putting God to the test, is the meaning of the name Massah; the fault-finding – with Moses in particular – is enshrined in the name Meribah. When the Lord later addressed the people with the unequivocal instruction quoted by Jesus, 'You shall not tempt the Lord your God,' he specifically reminded them of this earlier occasion – 'as you tested him at Massah' (Deut 6:16).

These two passages, the one from Exodus and the other from Deuteronomy, highlight the fundamental character of putting God to the test: it consists of a defiant, presumptuous or sometimes highly critical (i.e. critical of God) attitude which says, 'Is the Lord among us or not?' Calvin's phrase, just quoted, is most illuminating at this point: 'the neglect of those means which [God] puts into our hands'. That was precisely the problem at Massah, where they demanded that Moses provide water.

God had in fact shown the people, in many unprecedented ways, how many resources he had placed in their hands – not simply in the series of miracles prior to and surrounding their exodus from Egypt, but in the provision of quails and manna on the journey (recorded in the previous chapter, Exod 16). The Lord was manifestly among them – including the actual provision of water at Marah a few weeks earlier, when they were in a similar situation (Exod 15:22–25). Yet the people of God wanted to force the Lord into action on their behalf, instead of quietly trusting in the provision of a God who had already revealed his grace and power in their lives, and who had promised to take them safely through the wilderness to their destination.

This was the same temptation Satan launched across the path of Jesus in his wilderness. Jesus was completely willing to face the peril of death and to trust God to deliver him – but

only at God's command, in God's time and in God's way. He
knew that his Father had promised this deliverance to him; he
did not need to put that promise to the test. He accepted it and
lived in its complete trustworthiness, so that, on several
occasions in his next three years of ministry, he walked with
quiet confidence along the precipice of death, because he
knew that 'his hour had not yet come' (cf. John 7:30; 8:20).
When it did come, he bowed his meek head to mortal pain.

God has provided his sons and daughters in every generation with similar promises and similar resources. Above all,
we have the promise of Jesus: 'Lo, I am with you always, even
to the close of the age' (Matt 28:20). The Lord is among us,
and we put him to the test when, like his people in the
wilderness, we adopt any attitude which either doubts it or
demands that he prove it –either to us or to anyone else. After
winning over this temptation, Jesus steadily refused to perform signs in order to prove who he was (Emmanuel, 'God
with us', 'the Lord among us') or to prove what he could do,
so that men and women might be compelled to believe (cf.
Matt 12:38–42; 16:1–4; Luke 11:16; John 2:19; 6:30). In
essence, Jesus always answered such pressure by pointing
people again to himself (as the replies to the two questions in
John's gospel demonstrate, John 2:18–21; 6:30–35).

Defiant unbelief

We can fall foul of this temptation to put God to the test in
several ways. We can adopt a defiant attitude: 'I am not going
to believe God for this or that, unless he proves he is around
and alive.' Such an attitude is not restricted to unbelievers; as
Christians, we sometimes cling tenaciously to similar unbelief. We choose not to believe, for example, that God can
intervene miraculously in his world – either in judgment
through a fire at York Minster, or in guidance through
supernatural means (an angel, a dream, a vision), or in the
healing of a terminal or temporary illness. God has made it
plain, both in the promises written in the scriptures and in the
facts of human experience, that he is well able to act in these
ways. But we react, often with a sophisticated veneer of either

scientific or theological rationalism, by virtually defying God to prove it to us personally. We ignore what he has said and done; instead of trusting and obeying him, we demand a sign from heaven to show that the Lord is thus among us. And when we receive one, we can still persist in defiant unbelief.

I can recall, for example, an English clergyman who visited South America in the late 1970s. He saw remarkable examples of physical healing in profusion. They were neither spasmodic nor superficial, and there was on-the-spot corroboration by the medical profession. But back in the cagey scepticism of the (then fairly depressed) English church, he wrote an article for a Christian newspaper which essentially expressed unbelief. He was extremely sceptical about the Lord's being among his people to heal and perform such miracles. He needed more evidence, he wrote. That is putting the Lord to the test: what more evidence did he need or could he have been given?

Miracles to order

At the other end of the spectrum is the temptation to take a presumptuous attitude to God, one which requires him to perform miracles to order. Strangely, this attitude starts with no doubt at all in the ability of God to demonstrate his power in this way. It then slips, usually imperceptibly, into demanding that God prove his power to meet our needs, timetable or desires. There is a thin dividing line between this presumptuousness and genuine faith in the Lord. Perhaps an important clue is to be found in the attitude taken up if God does *not* respond to our faith-requests. If we do not receive what we ask – either for ourselves or for others – does our faith diminish? Or do we look around for scapegoats, those who did not have enough faith? In either reaction we could be revealing that we have been putting the Lord to the test, by requiring him to act in accordance with our wishes rather than trusting him to work in line with his promises and his wise love.

Calvin's comment about neglecting the means which God

has put into our hands is again helpful at this point. Frequently we request – or require – God to do something in a dramatic, miraculous or unusual way, when the means to do it lie already in our own hands. Every preacher, for example, knows the difference between, on the one hand, asking the Lord to undertake for us in power when we have been genuinely prevented from getting down to thorough preparation, and, on the other hand, walking into the pulpit on a song and a prayer when we have wasted preparation time in front of the TV or in bed. This latter kind of prayer is putting God to the test. The Lord is not committed to redeeming laziness, even if it is cloaked with wordy piety.

This may well be true also over the healing question. At its most basic level, God is unlikely to clear our nose and soothe our throat 'supernaturally' if he has already provided the means for such relief in the bathroom cabinet. Of course, he often does bring relief without such means: he is certainly able to do so. As medical science and technology continue to progress, the extent of these means becomes daily more and more remarkable. Where these resources are available, they are to be used – not automatically or without recourse to prayer, but with profoundly grateful prayer and also with the constant readiness to receive God's healing without medical means. This principle can be seen more accurately, perhaps, by looking at the extreme attitudes adopted by cults (like the Jehovah's Witnesses) whose adherents refuse blood transfusions or even (in the most extreme sects, as with some Christian Scientists) any medical means, even in emergencies. All such attitudes result in our putting the Lord to the test in a presumptuous way.

Putting the blame on God

A third way in which we often yield to the temptation in which Jesus found victory is when we find ourselves, like the Israelites in the wilderness, in extremely difficult and miserable circumstances. It is easy to fall into an attitude which throws all the blame on the Lord: 'You've got us into this mess, Lord: you will have to get us out.' This measure of

unbelief seems to be quite common among the many casu-
alties of the attitude previously described as presumptuously
holding a gun to God's head, requiring him to do a miracle.
When he does not perform to order, we throw the book at
him. We feel inside us that the Lord is no longer among us and
we challenge him to prove himself by taking us out of our
wretched situation. If he does not do what we want, we toss in
the towel.

The tragedy in such an attitude is that it prevents us from
recognising and receiving his love within the present situation. We are unable to recall the many promises which
guarantee his presence and grace in the midst of the very
worst that can happen. We make the improvement of our
circumstances the condition of trusting God, instead of – like
Habakkuk – trusting God whatever our circumstances:

> Though the fig tree do not blossom,
>   nor fruit be on the vines,
> the produce of the olive fail
>   and the fields yield no food,
> the flock be cut off from the fold
>   and there be no herd in the stalls,
> yet I will rejoice in the Lord,
>   I will joy in the God of my salvation.
> God, the Lord, is my strength;
>   he makes my feet like hinds' feet,
>   he makes me tread upon my high places.
>   (Hab 3:17–19)

When, therefore, we turn in a critical spirit on God and
demand that he must change our situation, we are putting him
to the test.

Calvin summarises the relevance for Christian disciples of
this second temptation to Jesus in the wilderness in the
following words: 'whoever desires to make an experiment of
the divine power, when there is no necessity for it, tempts
God by subjecting his promises to an unfair trial'.[10] Jesus
resolutely refused to snatch at power in this way. Had he done
so, bystanders would undoubtedly have been impressed – but
they would not have become believers. More than that, they

would have been given not a revelation of the character of God but a parody and a perversion. When Christians put God to the test today, the most serious result is that others are presented with a parody of the character of God and a perversion of the truth of God.

When God has made known his purposes, will and character – that in Jesus he truly is the Lord among us – we put him to the test when we doubt his power, demand proofs or deny his presence. After several false starts and personal blunders, Peter saw this very clearly when, at the council of Jerusalem, the admission of Gentile believers to the church was under discussion. God had manifestly grafted these believers into his church by 'giving them the Holy Spirit just as he did to us [Jews]; and he made no distinction between us and them, but cleansed their hearts by faith' (Acts 15:8–9). When Judaisers tried to foist on Gentile Christians not only circumcision but complete obedience to the law of Moses, Peter replied: 'why do you put God to the test by putting a yoke upon the neck of the disciples . . . ?' (Acts 15:10). The Judaisers were not prepared to accept the work of the Holy Spirit as evidence of the Lord being present in Gentile believers: they wanted *more* evidence before accepting them. Their sceptical and presumptuous behaviour seriously put the Lord to the test.

Avoiding the cross

The last temptation is probably the most unsubtle and yet most alluring of the three. It is, at one level, the temptation 'to achieve power by the worship of God's rival'.[11] At another less obvious but more searching level it is the first of many attempts by Satan to divert Jesus from the way of the cross. In the eternal plan of God – Father, Son and Holy Spirit – Jesus was to enter into his full sovereignty; every knee would bow to him, and every tongue would confess him Lord. But the road to glory went via Calvary. That required complete submission to the Father as the way to receiving his position of 'all authority in heaven and on earth' (Matt 28:18). Satan tempted him to snatch at this power prematurely: 'All these I will give you, if you will fall down and worship me' (Matt 4:9). The force of the temptation lay not in what Satan offered but in what would thereby be bypassed: suffering – the suffering of the cross and all that was to be involved in the three years leading up to the cross; the suffering of taking up his cross daily, denying himself and saying yes to the Father's will.

Paul in Philippians 2 stresses the way Jesus took the form of a servant: 'he humbled himself and became obedient unto death, even death on a cross' (Phil 2:8). Jesus submitted to his Father's will in complete obedience. It was this submissive obedience that Satan was attempting to undermine in this temptation, in precise parallel to his assault on the obedience of the first Adam. Satan's insatiable desire to command the worship of men and women is, of course, explicit and uppermost in the narrative: '. . . if you will fall down and worship me' (Matt 4:9). In this pride he has always overreached himself. Jesus was learning as a man to be an obedient servant, submissive to his Father in everything. This was integral to the mission of the Messiah, the suffering servant described especially in Isaiah. Satan attempted to drive a wedge between the messianic roles of suffering servant and future king, promising kingly authority without personal suffering. Jesus could have capitulated to this temptation only by breaking away from his submission to the will of God.

Because Jesus 'learned obedience through what he suffered' (Heb 5:8), he ultimately received what the devil promised him – and more – without bowing the knee to Satan: 'Therefore God has highly exalted him and bestowed on him the name which is above every name, that at the name of Jesus every knee should bow' (Phil 2:9–10). Equality with God was a matter of not snatching, especially when the enemy of God and man was applying the pressure to do precisely that. When Satan behaves in this way, he is acting in complete consistency with his own nature: equality with God was exactly what Satan wanted to snatch for himself. He is a snatcher, whereas the Lord is a giver. Satan was, therefore, trying to make Jesus like himself. He has consistently tried to misrepresent God, to make God look like himself – a greedy, grasping, restricting, depriving taker.

Who rules the world?

We need at this stage to ask whether Satan's claim to possess, and therefore to be able to dispense, 'all the kingdoms of the world and the glory of them' (Matt 4:8) was an accurate one. Was this power over the world his to give, or not? We will see later that this is an important question, because in its answer is contained a central truth about the nature of all earthly power and authority.

If this power is Satan's to wield and to dispense, then all human power of whatever kind has been contaminated by his dirty hands. Presumably this remains true even today, *after* the achievement of Jesus in destroying all the works of the devil. As in every area of our lives, Jesus' work of salvation and redemption needs to be applied and exercised wherever human power is being exerted.

If on the other hand Satan's claim was a hollow one, it is equally important to lay this bare, in order that the ways in which his sway is still exercised may be thoroughly exposed as futile. In this case the victory of Jesus over Satan, initially in the wilderness and ultimately through his death and resurrection, is to be seen primarily as the exposure of Satan's deceits and dupes rather than the termination of any actual power over the world. This could well be the force of Paul's teaching in Colossians 2:15, where the phrase rendered 'made a public example of them' could well mean 'exposed their true nature'. Alternatively we could see Satan's power to consist essentially of this deceit, i.e. his success in 'conning' men and women into believing that he is in control of the world.

Whichever conclusion we reach – that Satan's worldly power is real or that it is pretended – it is clear that Satan's temptation of Jesus along these lines held extremely attractive allure. For Jesus to claim his kingdom and enter his glory, 'Was it not necessary that the Christ should suffer . . . ?' (Luke 24:26). As Plummer puts it:

> That means a long and painful contest, involving much suffering to the Messiah and His followers. Why not have Satan for an ally instead of an enemy? Then sovereignty over Israel and all the nations may be quickly won, without

pain or trouble. With wealth, fashion, rank, intellect, intrigue, and force on His side, all backed by mighty works, success will be rapid and certain. A triumphant progress to supreme power . . . is offered to Him.[12]

The implicit message of Matthew and Luke's narratives of the temptations suggests strongly that Satan *did* possess the power which he offered Jesus. The devil 'claims a dominating influence over the world, which Jesus does not dispute'.[13] More clear still is the Johannine description of Satan as 'the ruler of this world' (John 12:31; 16:11), a title which Jesus uses of his adversary on the eve of his own death. He declares on that last night, as Judas brings soldiers to the garden of Gethsemane to conclude the business of betrayal, 'this is your hour, and the power of darkness' (Luke 22:53). These events all refer to the time before the crucifixion, which in John's gospel is perceived as the time when 'the Son of man [is] glorified, and in him God is glorified' (John 13:31; cf. 12:23). But half a century later, with the gospel road well travelled and the growth of the church established throughout most of the Mediterranean world, John still talks of Satan in these terms: 'We know that . . . the whole world is in the power of the evil one' (1 John 5:19; cf. Paul's description of Satan as 'the god of this world' in 2 Cor 4:4).

We conclude, therefore, that Satan did indeed exercise authority over all the kingdoms of the world; that their power and their glory was within his capacity to offer to Jesus (on his own terms); that Jesus acknowledged the reality both of his control over the world and of his power as tempter in this matter. Equally we conclude that Satan's power contained – and contains – a substantial element of deceit: he was fully aware that he had usurped God's authority; that his power was limited both in scope and in time; that the very one whom he was tempting was to be his ultimate conqueror. In brief, 'Satan is never absolute in his power. Whatever demands he makes, he can never exceed the boundaries set for him by God.'[14]

Whatever exactions Satan makes, and whatever temptations he brings, he still operates under the direct, specific sovereignty of God. Recognising him, therefore, as 'the ruler

of this world', even acknowledging the fact that 'the whole
world is in the power of the evil one', we can still both resist
him in firm faith and progressively reclaim, in the name of
Jesus, the kingdoms of this world from the usurper for their
proper Lord. Such a ministry requires from us, however, the
same refusal which Jesus made to evade the way of the cross,
the same willingness to lay down our lives in daily self-denial
and suffering, the same steady obedience to the will and word
of God our Father.

The road which Jesus walked

When we try to walk away from or around this suffering,
we have succumbed to the devil's third temptation: we want
the power and the glory without the suffering. We have
then come to regard equality with God as something to be
snatched, grabbed, grasped. Our greed and our impatience
betray the character of God which Jesus by his Spirit wants to
reproduce in us. It is sometimes argued that the power
available to us through the resurrection of Jesus and the gift of
the Spirit has taken us beyond the cross, both historically and
spiritually: we are 'King's kids' and can claim the resources of
the kingdom without the suffering which Jesus had to endure.
After all, it is argued, he went through all that so that we need
not go through it; we live on the other side of the cross; in his
love for us Jesus does not want us to suffer in any way.

This is obviously close to the truth; but it does not tally with
the truth as we see it in Jesus and hear it from Jesus. The devil
specialises in approximations to the truth; the closer he can
come while still obscuring the truth, the better he feels, and
the more persuasive his temptations. The ideas we have just
considered might be acceptable at one level, were it not for
the explicit *imitatio Christi* in the teaching of Jesus himself.
Consider these sayings: 'A disciple is not above his teacher,
nor a servant above his master; it is enough for the disciple to
be like his teacher, and the servant like his master' (Matt
10:24–25); 'A disciple is not above his teacher, but every one
when he is fully taught will be like his teacher' (Luke 6:40); 'I
have given you an example, that you also should do as I have

done to you. Truly, truly, I say to you, a servant is not greater than his master; nor is he who is sent greater than he who sent him. If you know these things, blessed are you if you do them' (John 13:15–17); 'Remember the word that I said to you, "A servant is not greater than his master." If they persecuted me, they will persecute you; if they kept my word, they will keep yours also' (John 15:20).[15]

We can add to these sayings the teaching of Jesus about the true nature of discipleship, especially as epitomised in those awesome phrases 'cannot be my disciple' and 'is not worthy of me'. Consider, for example, these words: 'He who loves father or mother more than me is not worthy of me; and he who loves son or daughter more than me is not worthy of me; and he who does not take his cross and follow me is not worthy of me' (Matt 10:37–38); 'If any one comes to me and does not hate his own father and mother and wife and children and brother and sisters, yes, and even his own life, he cannot be my disciple. Whoever does not bear his own cross and come after me, cannot be my disciple . . . whoever of you does not renounce all that he has cannot be my disciple' (Luke 14:26–27, 33). The first group was addressed to the twelve, the second to the multitudes: there is no distinction. The terms of discipleship have not altered. The way to our inheritance is the same as it was then, and our proper response is expressed succinctly by Paul: 'we rejoice in our hope of sharing the glory of God. More than that, we rejoice in our sufferings . . .' (Rom 5:2–3).

Developing the character of Jesus

Indeed, as Paul expands this theme, we can see plainly that the hope of glory and the experience of suffering have an even more integral connection than one might suspect: 'we rejoice in our sufferings, knowing that suffering produces endurance, endurance produces character, and character produces hope, and hope does not disappoint us, because God's love has been poured into our hearts through the Holy Spirit which has been given to us' (Rom 5:3–5). The thrust of this passage indicates that God gives us his Spirit so that his love in our hearts might strengthen us for the suffering which is intrinsic to Christian discipleship. As his love thus nerves and controls us, we are able to press forward through everything, without being diverted along the easy short cuts suggested by Satan. This endurance gradually writes into us true character, the character of Jesus. From his character being recreated within us comes the vibrant hope of glory, not the hope which (though cloaked in the language of heaven) is actually grounded in material blessings of a very earthly kind, but the hope of sharing the glory of God in the untrammelled fullness of eternal life.

It may not, therefore, be coincidental that endurance and character – the endurance and the character of Jesus – are seldom the obvious hallmarks of those today who adopt and advocate unrelieved 'prosperity teaching'. Deriving in origin, as it does, from Western (especially American) affluence, it produces disciples who reflect the traits of its cultural origins: concentration on instant results; petulance and capitulation when the going is tough; fragility under pressure; an unwillingness if not an outright refusal to look honestly at failure, weakness and sin – all in all, a mirror image of contemporary society instead of a faithful portrayal of the character of Jesus. In particular, power is seen in terms of getting it, maintaining it and extending it, not in terms of giving, sharing and serving. When this is applied by Christians to political and other secular power, it becomes a frightening parody of the power exercised by Jesus and incumbent on his disciples.

The way of the world

Many Christians pushing for political power in the USA, at local and national levels, are explicitly and unashamedly adopting the tactics and methods not merely of the market-place but of their opponents: 'If they can do it, so can we.'

Os Guinness has made a profound and searching critique of this phenomenon. He identifies four ways in which such Christians operate: dependency on conspiracy theories (all anti-God forces are deliberately ganging up on the true church – i.e. us); depiction in absolutist terms of good and evil (we are good, they are evil, and there is nothing in between); denial of free speech (shouting down the opposition and trying to prevent their voice being heard); and defamation of character (using every possible means to blacken the names of the opposition). Guinness describes these methods in turn as irrational, simplistic, intolerant and immoral.[16] Such a route to power has nothing to do with the way of Jesus, who was offered it by Satan and rejected it. It is a way which sidesteps the implications as well as the reality of the cross. It presumes to obtain what God wants without being prepared to walk the way Jesus walked. It is particularly subtle and dangerous when it is adopted by those with political power and then preached as being what God wants and as indicating that 'God is on our side.'

This kind of power, and the use of it, has been classically demonstrated by the apartheid regime in South Africa. Having lived in the USA for almost a year, including the time of the presidential election in November 1984, I can sense a similar attitude in that country's present administration. I am not concerned with the specific nature of its policies so much as with the God-talk which frequently permeates its public pronouncements and, in particular, its justification of much-debated priorities. This language reached its nadir when Mr Reagan claimed the backing of the Bible for the astonishing proliferation of the American nuclear arsenal, in particular of MX missiles. He quoted the words of Jesus, 'What king, going to encounter another king in war, will not sit down first and take counsel whether he is able with ten thousand to meet him who comes against him with twenty thousand?' (Luke 14:31). On that basis, asserted the President, the USA must match the Russians missile with missile, bomb with bomb – and actually work (and spend) for superiority.

There may of course be room for pragmatic argument about the wisdom of national defence through nuclear weaponry, but it is remarkably inept and arrogant to claim that Jesus is on your side. The end of the passage about the man building the tower and the king going to war actually contains the words we have already quoted: 'So therefore, whoever of you does not renounce all that he has cannot be my disciple' (Luke 14:33). So, far from enabling the President of the USA to claim that Jesus is on his side, Jesus is telling him that he cannot be a disciple of Jesus unless he renounces everything on which he is so clearly relying for power. Yet he is constantly invoking 'God bless America' and every dollar-bill declares 'In God we trust'. Is this not the classic capitulation to the devil's third temptation – to gain power over 'all the kingdoms of the world and the glory of them' not by walking the way of Jesus, to and through the cross, but by subscribing to the devil's methods and thereby submitting to the devil's conditions: '. . . if you will fall down and worship me'?

We will examine later whether Jesus expected the secular powers that be to operate completely in accordance with his own understanding and revelation of the true power of God, i.e. by not-snatching, but serving. At this stage we can surely affirm that if anyone (wherever they live and whoever they are) claims that God is on their side and simultaneously advocates methods and policies which sidestep the way of the cross, then that person has taken on board the devil's way of doing things. We all succumb to this temptation in various ways; but let us not fool ourselves about what is happening. We dare not call evil good and good evil, especially in the matter of power.

The seriousness of this struggle can perhaps best be seen in the apocalyptic but penetrating vision of John in the book of Revelation:

> Now war arose in heaven, Michael and his angels fighting against the dragon; and the dragon and his angels fought, but they were defeated and there was no longer any place for them in heaven. And the great dragon was thrown down, that ancient serpent, who is called the Devil and Satan, the deceiver of the whole world – he was thrown down to the death, and his angels were thrown down with him. And I heard a loud voice in heaven, saying: 'Now the salvation and the power and the kingdom of our God and the authority of his Christ have come, for the accuser of our brethren has been thrown down, who accuses them day and night before our God. And they have conquered him by the blood of the Lamb and by the word of their testimony, for

they loved not their lives even unto death. Rejoice then, O heaven and you that dwell therein! But woe to you, O earth and sea, for the devil has come down to you in great wrath, because he knows that his time is short!' (Rev 12:7–12)

When Jesus replied to the devil's third temptation with the peremptory command, 'Begone, Satan!' (Matt 4:10), he was anticipating the victory cry of Calvary, 'It is finished' (John 19:30), consummated in his glorious resurrection. At that point in history the power of Satan was essentially defeated and broken. We who live on earth, but with our citizenship in heaven, have 'the authority of God's Christ' to resist him, even in his 'great wrath'. The salvation and the power and the kingdom of our God have indeed come, revealed and restored in Jesus. It is a power and a kingdom of self-emptying, of serving, of suffering, of no-snatching.

The only other recorded occasion on which Jesus was forced to speak so bluntly to the devil, 'Begone, Satan!', was in rebuking Simon Peter for trying to divert him from the cross (Matt 16:23). This rebuke followed immediately on his pronouncement of special blessing on Peter (Matt 16:13–20), for being on the receiving end of clear revelation from God about the true identity of Jesus as 'the Christ, the Son of the living God'. Such revelation of Jesus and such testimony to Jesus is the raw material with which God builds his church. Satan can do nothing about that; but he can still undermine the witness of the church to her Lord by luring Christians away from the way and the significance of the cross. When Luke records that the devil 'departed from [Jesus] until an opportune time' (Luke 4:13), he is probably indicating that the substance of all three temptations would continue to challenge Jesus throughout his ministry.

3 SUCH PEOPLE ARE DANGEROUS –
POWER UNDER CONTROL

Immediately after the temptations in the wilderness, 'Jesus returned in the power of the Spirit into Galilee' (Luke 4:14). With these words Luke makes it plain that Jesus' victory over the devil established him in the power of the Holy Spirit in an unique way. The Spirit had descended upon him 'in bodily form, as a dove' in the Jordan (Luke 3:22). Then, 'full of the Holy Spirit', he had been 'led by the Spirit for forty days in the wilderness, tempted by the devil' (Luke 4:1–2). Now he began to minister 'in the power of the Spirit'. In the next two or three chapters, Luke mentions the ways in which this power was demonstrated. Three are explicitly described.

First, 'he taught in their synagogues' and 'they were astonished at his teaching, for his word was with authority' (Luke 4:15, 32). Secondly, 'he rebuked [the demons], and would not allow them to speak' (Luke 4:41) – with the result that 'they were all amazed and said to one another . . . "with authority and power he commands the unclean spirits, and they come out"' (Luke 4:36). Thirdly, 'the power of the Lord was with him to heal' and 'power came forth from him and healed them all' (Luke 5:17; 6:19). Luke's narrative leaves us with little room to evade the conclusion that this power from God was unleashed because he refused to exercise it in a selfish, spectacular or secular manner.

The gospel writers consistently hold together the healing ministry of Jesus and his teaching ministry (this is particularly true in John's gospel). In this way we are presumably intended to appreciate the inextricable bond between these two thrusts of his ministry. The power apparent in both was of a piece: it derived from his total submission to his Father, not only in pursuing his will but also in pursuing that will in God's way. The power of the Spirit filled him as a result. There was, therefore, nothing automatic in this power. The power was directed towards bringing men and women to the same integration and wholeness which he knew himself: i.e. to the same submission to God as Father, the same consecration to the Father's will, the same experience of the Spirit's power, the same security in the Father's love.

The authority of his teaching

The authority and impact of his teaching were the result of Jesus' complete commitment to bringing this message of wholeness (or salvation). He taught with the authority of God himself and he spoke as one who lived out what he was teaching. This was where he was so utterly different from the Jewish teachers of the law, the scribes and the Pharisees. They did not speak with God's authoritative voice; they were constantly quoting this, that and the other 'authority' – like preachers quoting scholarly comments and books rather than expounding God's word in the scriptures. Equally, they laid extremely heavy burdens on the ordinary people, without lifting a finger to show how to carry them: 'they don't practise what they preach. They tie on to people's backs loads that are heavy and hard to carry, yet they aren't willing even to lift a finger to help them carry those loads' (Matt 23:3–4 GNB).

The authority of Jesus came through his identification with the people, teaching them the way and the will and the word of God by submitting to it himself and coming alongside them in discovering what this submission meant in daily life. If we break up the wholeness of Jesus' life – seen in his teaching, healing and deliverance of people from demons – we no longer have a gospel or a saviour. The power of the Spirit came upon him so that he might demonstrate and impart his wholeness:

The Spirit of the Lord is upon me,
because he has anointed me to preach good news to the
  poor.
He has sent me to proclaim release to the captives

and recovering of sight to the blind,
to set at liberty those who are oppressed,
to proclaim the acceptable year of the Lord.

(Luke 3:18–19)

If people like the Pharisees and their scribes did not want to
know about this good news of wholeness and integration,
then the attitude of Jesus was unequivocal: 'Those who are
well have no need of a physician, but those who are sick; I
have not come to call the righteous, but sinners to repentance'
(Luke 5:31–32).

His teaching ministry was devoted to making these things
plain. It steadily painted a sharp contrast between worldly
standards and worldly ideas of power and the powerful, and
God's way and God's kind of power. This is never more clear
than in Matthew 5–7, the sermon on the mount, or in the
similar teaching in Luke's sermon on the plain (Luke 6:20–
49). The central theme of both sermons, which presumably
encapsulate teaching that was frequently on the lips of Jesus
in those three packed years, is the kingdom of God/heaven.
Although the detailed implications of this phrase are notoriously complex, it is theologically safe to affirm that it refers to
what happens when God's rule is in operation: i.e. the
characteristics of the kingdom and the character of the king.
We will see that, in this fundamental teaching, Jesus is
spelling out precisely the same truth about the nature of true
power as he has demonstrated with the devil in the wilderness: that it does not consist in grabbing what we can, in
manipulating people and events to meet our own desires, or in
attempting to force God's hand. Rather it involves giving
ourselves away, not snatching at what we might legitimately
claim for ourselves. It involves allowing our attitudes and
actual character to be gradually moulded into the pattern of
our Father God himself – 'You . . . must be perfect, as your
heavenly Father is perfect' (Matt 5:48). With such open and
growing Christians God can safely move in establishing his
kingdom, not least in powerful demonstrations of healing and
deliverance.

We will, therefore, take a closer look at the message of the sermon on the mount, particularly as it relates directly to the theme of Jesus and power. The beatitudes and the Lord's prayer are especially relevant.

The sermon on the mount

The overall message of the sermon can be summarised as follows: the sons and daughters of God the Father must regard as top priority *his* rule and *his* character, i.e. they must seek first his kingdom and his righteousness; in so doing they will demonstrate their utter distinctiveness from the rest of mankind. The disciples of Jesus are to be different, as different and distinctive as he was. The beatitudes' eight characteristics of truly happy or blessed people are a perfect description of Jesus: poor in spirit, mourning (for sin), meek, hungering and thirsting for righteousness, merciful, pure in heart, making peace, and persecuted as a result by those whose ideas and pursuit of worldly power made them suspicious, resentful and scared of such a distinctive kind of unconquerable power. 'The message of the Beatitudes . . . is first and foremost a message about Christ and his kingdom. The Beatitudes reveal what God is, not just what we should be. They teach us what the kingdom of God is, and not just what we must do in order to enter it.'[1]

Specific beatitudes seem directly to echo the experiences of Jesus under temptation in the wilderness. Was he hungry and being lured into turning stones into bread? He had a much deeper and all-consuming hunger for true righteousness, *God's* righteousness. Was he under pressure from Satan to put God to the test and to doubt whether God's promise would genuinely hold good? He retained absolute purity of heart before God. Was he being inveigled into using his power in a self-assertive and manipulative fashion? He maintained an attitude of submissive meekness, remaining poor in spirit instead of using his God-given power in a triumphalistic manner. That was the way to true blessedness before his Father in heaven. That was the way to establish the kingdom of God among men and women, to 'inherit the earth'. In this lifestyle of no-snatching he found complete comfort and satisfaction as the Son of God, keeping before him the vision of God as sovereign Lord.

The way for his disciples is no different. Equally, that way was full of opposition, ridicule and persecution for him, so it will be for his disciples also (Matt 5:11–12). That is the way of righteousness; it is utterly distinctive (Matt 5:13–16) and it reaches deep down into our hearts, into the very mainsprings of our thoughts, our ambitions, our desires and our motives (Matt 5:17–20). The authentic power of true righteousness, on the pattern of Jesus, emerges as we are changed in the inner core of our being – where anger is kindled (Matt 5:21–26), where lust lies (Matt 5:27–32), where falsehood and lying lurk (Matt 5:33–37), where resentment can spawn retaliation (Matt 5:38–42), and where preoccupation with self gives rise to calculated kindness (Matt 5:43–47) – with one eye on what we can get out of it, instead of unconditional generosity after the example and character of our 'heavenly Father' (Matt 5:48).

Such distinctive and radical righteousness is not merely opposed to any paraded piety (Matt 6:1), it is actively committed to a 'secret' spirituality – in matters like giving money (Matt 6:2–4), praying (Matt 6:5–13) and fasting (Matt 5:16–18) – a spirituality grounded in such a deep experience of God's undeserved forgiveness that we extend unconditional forgiveness to others, *all* others (Matt 6:14–15). It has learnt detachment from the greedy power of money (Matt 6:19–24) and the neurotic worry that invariably rides in on the back of affluence (Matt 6:25–34). It recognises that the problems of the world lie within my own heart, not with the sins of others (Matt 7:1–6). The heart is the source of everything: if I am wrong there, I am inevitably wrong elsewhere – if not everywhere (Matt 7:15–20). God's will is focused on my heart, my inner being: will I ask and let him deal with me there (Matt 7:7–11)? No amount of sound doctrine or impressive ministry can replace that radical surgery (Matt 7:21–23). I am a fool if I think otherwise (Matt 7:24–27). It's a hard road to travel, but it is the only one that leads to life (Matt 7:13–14).

This is what Jesus preached, and this is what Jesus practised: it is not surprising, on reflection, that 'when Jesus finished these sayings, the crowds were astonished at his teaching' (Matt 7:28). Neither the message nor the preacher bore any resemblance to their own teachers and scribes, however much influence and authority they obviously exercised over ordinary folk. Having withstood the temptations of Satan to use power less radically and less authentically, Jesus had the authority to teach these things to his disciples. In a strange but totally gripping way the unerring focus of the sermon on the mount is the preacher himself: here lies true power – with God and with men.

What is meekness?

There is one particular word in the third beatitude which provides a sharp insight into the nature and source of the power which Jesus exercised: the word 'meek'.[2] It is a word he specifically uses to describe himself: 'Take my yoke upon you, and learn from me; for I am meek and lowly in heart, and you will find rest for your souls' (Matt 11:29). This famous invitation is issued to 'all who labour and are heavy laden': 'Come to me,' he says, 'and I will give you rest.' Because this invitation is an unmistakable statement of the good news, it is important to understand a bit more of what it means to be meek. What is still more intriguing is that these 'comfortable words' (as the 1662 Book of Common Prayer describes them) are preceded immediately by a statement from the lips of Jesus, in which he claims virtual sovereignty over this world and the next: 'All things have been delivered to me by my Father; and no one knows the Son except the Father, and no one knows the Father except the Son and any one to whom the Son chooses to reveal him' (Matt 11:27).

Jesus follows this breathtaking assertion with the invitation to all weary people to come to him for rest: 'for I am meek'. Total authority is vested by God in this meek man from Nazareth who then offers rest to all who will come to him. What is this meekness? Part of the answer lies in the root meaning of the word. It was used originally of a horse, or some other wild animal, which had been broken in, tamed and was now useful to its owner. All its hitherto uncontrolled and unusable strengths were harnessed. Until they had been brought under control the animal was useless and even dangerous.

It is clear that this background to the word is present in the mind of Jesus when he describes himself as meek and invites the weary to come to him for rest. This is placed explicitly in the context of the instruction to take his yoke and to learn from him. The yoke kept animals under control and made them useful to their owner. Jesus seems to see discipleship in terms of submitting our strengths to the yoke he himself has accepted. Harnessed to him beneath that yoke of submission to our heavenly Father, we become useful to the Lord and we also, almost incidentally, find rest. Having lived willingly and at peace underneath that yoke for so long, Jesus wants to teach and train us for the same strength-in-submission. The verses which lead up to the invitation indicate strongly that this submission in the Godhead is a mutual submission of love – one which Jesus, the eternal Son of God, has known and embraced from eternity; one, moreover, which he will continue to practise into eternity. For this is the essence of both the love and the power of God.

The same picture is in the foreground when Jesus enters Jerusalem on a donkey on Palm Sunday. This is the King of kings coming to claim his kingdom – through rejection, suffering and death. Matthew's quotation (Matt 21:5) from the prophet Zechariah is completely appropriate and profoundly precise in its emphasis on power demonstrated in humble action:

> Rejoice greatly, O daughter of Zion!
> Shout aloud, O daughter of Jerusalem!
> Lo, your king comes to you:
> triumphant and victorious is he,
> meek and riding on an ass,
> on a colt the foal of an ass
> (Zech 9:9).

In the same passage of Zechariah, the impact of such a demonstration of such a kind of power is spelt out very vividly:

> I will cut off the chariot from Ephraim
> and the war horse from Jerusalem;
> and the battle bow shall be cut off,
> and he shall command peace to the nations;
> his dominion shall be from sea to sea,
> and from the River to the ends of the earth.
> (Zech 9:10).

In other words, all the emblems of worldly might and power will fall to this peacemaker who comes in meekness to establish righteousness – he will inherit the earth because he has learnt to let God control him and he is from the heart submitted to the kingly rule of the sovereign Lord.

Meekness, therefore, means power under control. The word came to hold immense significance for the apostles and for the early church. If we trace through the New Testament the occasions on which the word is used, we will see both how central and how practical is this application of power, given by God, now controlled by God and used for God. As such, it is seen as part of the fruit of the Spirit: it is not the natural disposition of a few courteous and good-mannered people. On the contrary, it is both impossible without the Holy Spirit and incumbent on all those who have received new life in the Spirit. The letter-writers of the New Testament mention seven distinct situations in which this meekness, power under control, is necessary for the disciples of the meek Jesus.

Meekness in Christians

First, Paul addresses the life of the local church in fellowship with one another. He urges the Colossians (Col 3:12) to put on meekness, along with several other essential qualities. In his letter to the Ephesians (Eph 4:2), he emphasises that Christians betray their calling when they fail to exercise forbearance with one another in all meekness and patience. We all have the power to contribute to the health of the body of Christ, but that power must be under the control of the Holy Spirit, demonstrated in eagerness to maintain unity in the bond of peace. Our strengths of character, personality and willpower need to be submitted to the Spirit of Jesus within us. God has entrusted to his church many such strengths for building good relationships with people. We must resist the temptation to use them in order to get our own way or to foster allegiance to ourselves.

I recently heard about one local church. New life had begun to flow, so one day a Christian in the vicinity, who had led an independent home-fellowship for several years, decided to join the church, along with the other people in the group. For several years, the strengths of this man and of his friends were used within the life of the church – but always with conditions, implicitly or explicitly stated. There was a basic lack of true submission both to the local fellowship and to its leadership. Eventually, the strengths of this small group became entrenched against the others, rather than alongside them, and they left the church. They were eager, not to maintain unity in the bond of peace, but to express their strengths and their gifts on their own terms – and that is lack of meekness. Unsubmitted strengths are dangerous in the family of God; they produce strife and division.

Second, in writing to Timothy, Paul urges his fairly timid protégé to exercise leadership at Ephesus in a non-quarrelsome way, particularly in his teaching ministry. He will find himself being opposed on any one of several issues, but he must learn the skill of 'correcting his opponents with meekness' (2 Tim 2:25). One particular strength which Timothy possessed was Paul's apostolic authority undergirding his leadership. Timothy would have been tempted to use this with the wrong kind of assertiveness: the less confident we are, the more tempted we are to pull rank. Paul will not countenance such a misrepresentation of the meekness shown by Jesus. In fact, in his difficult dealings with the sensitive Corinthians about their unwillingness to go along with his own apostolic authority, Paul bases his appeal to them on 'the meekness and gentleness of Christ' (2 Cor 10:1).

A third example of the need for meekness comes in the letter of James. He urges his readers to 'put away all filthiness and rank growth of wickedness and receive with meekness the implanted word, which is able to save your souls' (Jas 1:21). This instruction exposes our inner attitude to God's word, especially when it challenges any habits or attitudes which have ingrained ungodliness in our behaviour. We can then use our powers of critical judgment and independent thinking to place ourselves above the authority of God's word. We come to treat it as outmoded and irrelevant, instead of that which has the power to save our souls – if of course we submit to the incarnate Word who comes to us in the written word. This kind of meekness enables us to bring all our powers into the strenuous challenge of obeying God's word, not rationalising our rejection of its demands: 'be doers of the word, and not hearers only, deceiving yourselves' (Jas 1:22).

Meekness is required also – and fourthly – when we are approached by those who do not know Christ and are living without hope. Peter urges us always to be ready to give an answer to whose who question us about our hope of eternal life – but with a proviso, 'yet do it with meekness and reverence' (1 Pet 3:15). There is a strong temptation to come on strong and to become 'preachy' in such a situation. We have the immense advantage of knowing the truth as it is in Jesus; but we must not use that advantage in an aggressive, insensitive, patronising or manipulative way. It is all too easy to use our power wrongly at this highly sensitive point in a person's search for God. It may well have taken them much time and courage to reach this level of honest vulnerability about their personal hopelessness. We cannot afford to move ahead without the meekness of Jesus.

Equally, there will, fifthly, be occasions within the life of a church when a Christian brother or sister transgresses God's laws in a fairly blatant way. How should this be tackled? Paul tells the Galatians to ensure that such a delicate task is placed in the hands of those who can minister grace and truth 'in a spirit of meekness' (Gal 6:1). It is not difficult to come down on flagrant sin like a ton of bricks, with all the compacted power of biblical authority and church discipline – not to mention the impact of spiritual alienation from the fellowship of believers. Paul explains that one of the secrets of a proper meekness is the realistic awareness that even the most spiritual among us will be tempted in exactly the same way. The authority of Christ to administer reproof and correction must therefore be administered with the meekness of Christ. I

sometimes wonder how many cases of thorough church discipline would never have reached the stage requiring such
serious action if the initial approach to the Christian
concerned had been characterised by this meekness.

Sixthly, meekness is required in those to whom the Lord
has given the power to make wise decisions and to use words
effectively. In his famous chapter on the tongue, James
delineates in bold colours the way we can unleash such
terrible misery with such a little 'member'. He then proceeds
to talk of the proper use of our tongues (Jas 3:1–13, esp. 13).
We all need wisdom, and the Lord gives it – without any hint
of reproach or niggardliness – to those who humbly ask him.
But the gift of wisdom can be demonstrated without the
necessary context of a consistently 'good life'. It then becomes unconvincing because it lacks integrity. The wisdom of
the Lord is revealed by the meekness with which it is offered.
Much wisdom in Christians is of the kind which convinces us
of our ignorance. We feel overawed, not instructed.

Our seventh and final example of meekness in the New
Testament comes from the pen of Peter, who urges Christian
women with unconverted husbands to prize above all else 'the
imperishable jewel of a meek and quiet spirit, which in God's
sight is very precious' (1 Pet 3:4). Traditional understandings
of the word 'meek' would consign this text to the cultural
rubbish-heap in our age of equal rights and anti-chauvinism.
Properly interpreted, however, Peter's insistence on the pre-
eminent value of meekness becomes a very different matter.
A woman has immense strengths, unique qualities, great
gifts, and unparalleled power with her husband: if she can
learn quietly and confidently to let all these come under the
control of Jesus, God will be able to use this meekness to
win over her unbelieving husband. Such meekness is very
precious to God.

If, on the other hand, she adopts either a superior attitude
or an anxious evangelistic policy towards her husband, he will
either feel steamrollered into a passive acquiescence which
falls a long way short of true conversion, or he will run a mile.
The meekness of Jesus, if it can 'inherit the earth', can
certainly win the allegiance of an unconverted partner.

We can, then, readily appreciate why Paul contrasts an

approach which relies on 'the rod' with the way of love 'in a spirit of meekness' (1 Cor 4:21). The first method is the worldly way of exercising power – asserting, striving, compelling. The second way is the way in which Jesus exercised power, in submission to his heavenly Father and in dependence on the Spirit. The challenge of the third beatitude is underlined by the promise attached to it: 'Blessed are the meek, for they shall inherit the earth' (Matt 5:5). That flies in the face of all secular understanding of power, which essentially proclaims that only those who push and shove will get anywhere.

When Alexander Solzhenitsyn was in prison in Russia he came to realise that

> as long as he was trying to maintain some power – whether it was for food, clothing, or health – he was at the mercy of his captors. When he realised and accepted, and even embraced his powerlessness, then he became completely free; the power of his captors over him ceased. In the way of life's strange paradoxes, he became the powerful, they the powerless.[3]

The principles enshrined in Christian meekness are given flesh and blood in the rest of Jesus' teaching in the sermon on the mount. No wonder God's reign has been called 'the upside-down kingdom'.

> Thus we may say that the Beatitudes apply first of all to Christ – that Jesus is the sole 'Happy One,' and that, in Jesus, the Beatitudes are . . . the expression of his experience of the kingdom, and of his interior life. The Beatitudes reveal the true face of Christ – his criteria, his attitudes, and his loves . . . They reveal the attitudes Jesus had, and hence those his followers should have.[4]

The Lord's prayer

At the heart of the sermon on the mount we find what has come to be called 'the Lord's prayer' (Matt 6:9–13). Jesus' teaching about prayer is as distinctive and striking as the rest of his teaching. It seems clear that his disciples were particularly impressed, not by the mere fact that he prayed or even that he prayed frequently and lengthily, but by the facility and intimacy with God with which he prayed. They asked him to teach them to pray in that way. Luke's narrative, in the two or three chapters immediately following the story of his temptation, unmistakably links the power of the Spirit in Jesus with his habits of prayer (cf. Luke 4:42; 5:16; 6:12). It is most reasonable, therefore, to see in the Lord's prayer itself a revelation of the prayer life of Jesus and consequently an important clue to the secret of his power.

When we examine the Lord's prayer in this way, we can see a marked echo once again of his experiences in the wilderness in being tempted by the devil. Several, if not all, of the petitions appear to have direct application to specific details of the temptations. Is Jesus not teaching his disciples how he himself prayed in the Spirit during those forty pressurised days? Throughout the devil's temptations he determined to hallow God's name above all; to ensure that worship was directed to his Father, God, and not to any rival or usurper; and to apply himself totally to establishing God's kingdom. When tempted to gain his kingdom by methods and along avenues prohibited by the will of God, he rejected them unconditionally. Although hungry, he relied on his heavenly Father to feed him with true spiritual food – sufficient for his immediate needs.

Throughout that extended time of satanic pressure, Jesus had steadily adhered to the will of God, and to his calling to ensure that this will would be accomplished on earth. The phrase 'on earth as it is in heaven' is not simply a prayer that the earth might eventually come under the will of God in the same way as heaven now demonstrates his perfect will. It indicates the desire that God's will be established by methods which are in genuine accord with the character and heart of God. Jesus is as concerned with means as with ends; for him and for his disciples, the ends can never justify the means. That, as we have seen, was integral to his victory over the tempter.

We can see, therefore, that the first four petitions of the

prayer provide a window into Jesus' own communion in prayer with his Father during the temptation in the wilderness. The next two verses, Matthew 6:12–13, seem not to reflect the experience of Jesus. He had no need to ask for forgiveness, and Matthew has expressly stated that he was actually 'led up by the Spirit into the wilderness to be tempted by the devil' (Matt 4:1). Clearly there are differences between Jesus and ourselves at this point.

Yet these differences may not be as determinative as they appear. From the very fact that Jesus chooses to emphasise the priority of forgiveness (from God to us and from us out to others) in the next paragraph of the sermon (Matt 6:14–15), we can appreciate how central a place such all-embracing forgiveness holds in the kingdom of God. So much powerlessness in the church stems from continued guilt before God and persistent bitterness towards others. Jesus, on the other hand, enjoyed intimate security with his Father and was filled with compassion and mercy towards everyone – including those who opposed, ridiculed, persecuted, denied, betrayed or abandoned him. We can know the same security with God and compassion towards others, as the direct fruit of having been forgiven through the atoning death of Jesus.

What about the notorious problems surrounding the petition traditionally translated 'lead us not into temptation, but deliver us from evil'? The problems are notorious because scholarly uncertainty has found its way into modern liturgies, with variations on a theme such as, 'Do not bring us to the time of trial'. The second half of the petition seems most happily rendered 'deliver us from the evil one', mainly because 'Matthew's first mention of temptation (4:1–11) is unambiguously connected with the Devil'.[5] The double use of the word meaning 'into' (i.e. as a prefix for the verb meaning 'lead' and as a preposition before the noun translated 'temptation') suggests that this is a prayer to the Father for us to be so led by the Spirit that we do not fall when tempted, but are rescued both from the scheming and from the frontal assaults of the devil. A combination of traditional and modern would then give us the 'feel', if not the precise translation, of the petition in a paraphrase such as: 'Lead us, Lord, but not so far into temptation that we reach the place where we fall; rather,

ensure that we are rescued from the clutches of the evil
one.'

We are, in other words, *bound* to meet temptation –
particularly along the lines which the tempter used with Jesus.
We need strong leadership from God through his Spirit if we
are to tone our spiritual muscles in the face of such temptation, and thus develop true power in Jesus. As the sons and
daughters of our Father God, we need to let the Spirit lead us
through testing and precarious life-situations (cf. Rom 8:12–
17). Our power remains small if we stay on safe, comfortable
terrain. When Jesus moved out in the power of the Spirit, he
was led to places and people where oppression, blindness,
bondage and poverty reigned.

The Lord's prayer can be readily seen, therefore, as the
way Jesus was teaching his disciples to tap the source of true
power. On this analysis, it encapsulates the secret of his own
experience of God's power in the face of an internal and
protracted concentration of satanic pressure. If we take the
prayer as a model instead of as a mantra, we will find the
words of the doxology (which is almost certainly a later
addition to the original text) coming true in our own lives:
'For thine is the kingdom and the power and the glory, for
ever. Amen (Matt 6:13). The whole prayer is an act of
submission, bringing our lives into line with the will of God
the Father – acknowledging his uniqueness, recognising his
right to rule, presenting ourselves to be agents of his will,
depending on his gracious provision, sharing his free forgiveness, and asking for his direct leadership. To live each day like
that is to become free to walk as Jesus walked, to do what
Jesus did. We show the authentic marks of the kingdom of
God.

4 DON'T CROWD ME – POWER
WITH HIS FRIENDS

There is probably no single aspect of power more suspect or ambivalent than the power to influence people. History is full of vivid examples of the way one person can control not just the lives but the minds of millions – Muhammad, Marx, Hitler, Gandhi, Mao, Confucius. Power with people is a two-edged sword. In daily encounter in our own generation, one of the deepest cries of the human heart is for the freedom to be ourselves, i.e. for room to move and not to be manipulated or used by powerful people. That cry is no less profound or poignant in the democracies of the West than under repressive totalitarian regimes in other parts of the world. We are all instinctively on our guard against people with personal power to influence our own lives. Was Jesus any different? He exercises power today over more people than any other person in history – although to say 'over' people is misleading. Our first three chapters have underlined the stress in Jesus' life and teaching on the power to serve, not to dominate or control. This may turn out to be the key to his power with people. Let us look at the gospel narratives.

John the Baptist

Jesus' first encounter, in all four gospels, is with his cousin John the Baptist. In both their families the prophecies surrounding their births must have been matters of discussion and constant study. John was to be 'great before the Lord', to be 'filled with the Holy Spirit' and to be the forerunner of the Messiah 'in the spirit and power of Elijah' (Luke 1:15–17). His father Zechariah had said in prophecy that 'you, child,

will be called the prophet of the Most High' (Luke 1:76). John
was ready for a high-profile public ministry, as a preparation
for the Saviour to do his unique work among the people.
When he eventually began this preaching, 'a baptism of
repentance for the forgiveness of sins' (Luke 3:3), there was a
steely aggressiveness in his manner and message (cf. Luke
3:7–14). Nobody could mistake the directness of his message,
which stressed judgment on those who refused to repent.
John must have been a frightening man to meet. His ministry was confrontational and powerful, demanding and
dramatic.

He knew that he was only preparing the way for someone
'mightier than I, the thong of whose sandals I am not worthy
to stoop down and untie' (Mark 1:7). This far mightier person
would have a much more powerful ministry – 'I baptize you
with water . . . he will baptize you with the Holy Spirit and
with fire' (Luke 3:16). John obviously saw the ministry of
Jesus in terms of salvation for the believer and of judgment
for those who rejected him: 'His winnowing fork is in his
hand, to clear his threshing floor, and to gather the wheat into
his granary, but the chaff he will burn with unquenchable fire'
(Luke 3:17).

If so confrontational, if not abrasive, a personality as John
had such expectations of Jesus, it is surely no surprise that
John is startled by the demeanour and behaviour of Jesus at
their first public encounter by the river Jordan. Jesus, this far
mightier baptiser with the Holy Spirit in power to save and in
judgment, asks John to baptise him. This was the one whose
way he had been assiduously preparing. If anything, the boot
should be on the other foot; 'I need to be baptized by you'
(Matt 3:14) was his stunned reaction. The very first action of
the Lord is to humble himself, to submit to John, to express
total identification with sinners in their sinfulness. John cannot fathom such expression of supreme power, but he bows to
the authority of Jesus. When his disciples begin, at his own
exhortation, to transfer their allegiance to Jesus, John tes-
tifies to his joy. John likens his own role to that of the best man
to the bridegroom: 'He must increase, but I must decrease'
becomes his determination (John 3:29–30). Soon after, John
is thrown into prison by Herod, where he languishes, in

ever-decreasing morale, while the ministry and reputation of Jesus increase dramatically.

It seems probable that John had been in prison for over a year when he sent a message to Jesus questioning him whether he truly was the Messiah, 'or shall we look for another?' (Matt 11:3). The clarion certainty of his public ministry had understandably been eroded by his internment. Above all, the judgment he had proclaimed on those who rejected Jesus ('the chaff') had not materialised. There was mounting opposition to the kind of messiahship that Jesus was demonstrating; but where was the fire of God's judgment? What about the injustice of his own imprisonment and Herod's continuing reign of corruption and injustice?

Answering John's doubts

No wonder John doubted the wisdom, relevance and effectiveness of Jesus' approach to power. Jesus proceeded to respond to John's raging doubts in three distinct ways.

First, according to Luke, 'in that hour he cured many of diseases and plagues and evil spirits, and on many that were blind he bestowed sight' (Luke 7:21). As far as I can determine, this is the only occasion recorded in the gospels when Jesus went out on his own initiative to cure people. Having made sure that John's two disciples had taken due note of what he was doing, he sent them back to his imprisoned and depressed cousin with the instructions, 'Go and tell John what you have seen and heard: the blind receive their sight, the lame walk, lepers are cleansed, and the deaf hear, the dead are raised up, the poor have good news preached to them' (Luke 7:22). If John could understand only mightier demonstrations of the Spirit's power than he himself had performed, then in his extremity he must have them. Although John himself had not worked any mighty works (John 10:41), such miracles were signs of the kingdom of heaven on earth, however much they are open to misunderstanding and even if they can be a distraction from its true nature. John would have been able to see the marks of the Messiah in these miracles.

But Jesus' parting shot to John via his two disciples re-
focuses his cousin's attention on the heart of the gospel of the
kingdom: 'blessed is he who takes no offence at me' (Matt
11:6; Luke 7:23). John had been in danger of tripping over the
sheer grace, humility and servanthood at the heart of Jesus'
ministry. The niggling doubts, which had perhaps crossed his
mind right at the beginning by the river Jordan when Jesus
showed such unexpected submissiveness and meekness, rose
destructively to the surface in the loneliness of Herod's jail.[1]
How could the kingdom of God be established in such a
humble, self-denying fashion? It simply would not work.
Jesus sensitively gave the doomed John encouragement to
renewed faith; but quietly and firmly he also reaffirmed the
kind of Messiah he had been sent to be.

Jesus' second response to the doubts expressed by John was
directed to the crowds who had witnessed his encounter with
John's two disciples. After reassuring them that John was no
unreliable 'reed shaken by the wind' (Luke 7:24), fickle in his
allegiance to Jesus, he drew an implicit but clear contrast
between the sternly ascetic lifestyle of the prisoner and the
effeminate luxury of his captor Herod. Having reinstated
John in the popular mind as a true man of God, Jesus declared
that John was indeed a prophet 'and more than a prophet'
(Luke 7:26) – this was important, since there had been no
genuine prophet in Israel since Malachi, four hundred years
previously. Jesus then brought his eulogy of John to a climax
by saying, 'Truly, I say to you, among those born of women
there has risen no one greater than John the Baptist' (Matt
11:11; cf. Luke 7:28).

The next remark of Jesus again redresses any imbalance in
his genuine praise of John, 'yet he who is least in the kingdom
of heaven is greater than he' (Matt 11:11; Luke 7:28). The
vocabulary of 'least' and 'greatest' immediately brings to our
mind the various passages in the gospels where Jesus talks
about rank and precedence in the kingdom of God. Jesus saw
little children as both a pointer to and an example of the
kingdom's authentic trademarks (see chapter one). He also
pinpointed servanthood and self-humbling as essential
characteristics of his own ministry, and therefore of our own
ministry as his disciples.

Jesus must therefore have been referring, at least indirectly, to this 'bottom line' in the matter of entering the kingdom of heaven: we have to become like little children, acknowledge our unrelieved spiritual poverty before God, and be born all over again by the Spirit of God. If a person has travelled that narrow road and gone no further, he may be least in the kingdom of heaven – but he has entered the kingdom on his knees as a sinner, and that is the only way in.

Because of his unique vocation to be the forerunner of Jesus, John had lived and preached in advance of that gospel message. In pointing John away from his inner doubtings to Jesus' own credentials as the Christ, as the Saviour, as the Lamb of God who takes away the sins of the world (the substance of John's own earlier testimony to Jesus, John 1:29, 36), Jesus was nurturing such saving faith in his hesitant cousin.

We cannot but affirm that John the Baptist has his place in God's kingdom: but the ministry of the Saviour-Messiah at this crucial moment might well have been the actual time of release for this special captive (cf. Luke 4:18). Hitherto, John had been driven by a 'gung-ho' approach to the ungodly. That is fine, until the ungodly – such as Herod – seem to triumph. In his physical prison John found himself spiritually imprisoned by his own misconceived notions about the way God should operate. In this bondage Jesus brought inner freedom.

The third way in which Jesus responds to the doubts of John has come down to us as probably the least understood saying in the gospels. It would therefore be rash to base too solid an argument on such a difficult verse. It runs like this: 'From the days of John the Baptist until now the kingdom of heaven has suffered violence, and men of violence take it by force' (Matt 11:12). Donald Carson has an excellent discussion of 'this enigmatic saying',[2] concluding with what he regards as the best solution: from the time John began his ministry of getting God's people ready for the coming of the Messiah, right up until this particular point in the ministry of Jesus, 'the kingdom of heaven has been forcefully advancing; and violent or rapacious men have been trying . . . to plunder it'.[3] In other words, in Jesus the kingdom of God has been making immense strides, coming in power in people's lives. But this has provoked bitter opposition, opposition which will intensify from this point onwards and will culminate in the cross.

This violent opposition is 'the very point John could not grasp'.[4] The opposition 'was rising and would get worse'.[5] It is important to note at this stage (something Carson is very clear about) that the opposition came not just from those who wanted to get rid of Jesus but from those who wanted a strong political or even a military leader – i.e. from 'the materialism that craved a political Messiah and the prosperity he would bring but not his righteousness'.[6] Moreover, Carson sees the last few verses of Matthew 11 as indisputable evidence that Jesus was bent on opening the kingdom of God not to forceful, aggressive, powerful people who wanted to snatch at the blessings of God's kingdom, but to the weary and the heavy-laden who desperately wanted to find rest for their souls.[7] This kind of power, vested in the Son by the Father and at the very heart of the Son's ministry, was recognised only by 'babes' – i.e. by those who knew they depended completely on the Father's grace (see Matt 11:25–30).

It has been of fundamental importance to spend time on Jesus' approach to John the Baptist. John was an exceedingly strong person, the kind of man who finds it very difficult to go along with Jesus' pattern of no-snatching. John was unable to dismiss the claims of Jesus, even at the bottom of his morale and in the classic place of helplessness (in prison). That is where strong people are at last able to receive the pattern of power which Jesus demonstrated. Jesus always has to struggle with those who see power in worldly terms. His miracles often intensified that struggle. When, for example, he fed the five thousand with two loaves and five small fish, he perceived 'that they were about to come and take him by force to make him king' (John 6:15). He had to withdraw from the crowds to be by himself, simply to avoid being cast in the mould of an earthly king wielding worldly power.

No snatching

It is intriguing – and presumably not just coincidental – that the Greek word (*harpazō*) used in Matthew 11:12 and John

6:15 is the one translated 'grasped' or 'snatched' in Philippians 2:6. Jesus saw ultimate power in terms of no-snatching; but a corollary of John's ministry was to encourage forceful men to try to snatch at God's kingdom. Equally, because a miraculous provision of food for a hungry crowd held out hopes of freedom, prosperity and power for the Jews, they tried to snatch Jesus to become their kind of leader against the hated Romans. God's kingdom does not operate like that: none of us has the right to commandeer the kingdom for our own ends, either by using the name of Jesus to justify unchristian methods or by asserting that God is on our side in our particular worldly struggles.

Nowhere is the power of Jesus to affect others more clearly demonstrated than in his life with the twelve disciples. The evangelists between them provide details of his initial call of seven: Simon and Andrew, James and John, Philip, Bartholomew (or Nathanael) and Matthew (or Levi) (cf. Matt 4:18–22; John 1:35–51; Luke 5:27–28). In virtually every case (Bartholomew seems to be the exception) the summons of Jesus was simple and total: 'Follow me.' From that moment they left behind everything they possessed, in order to follow Jesus in his itinerant ministry. They also left their family and friends. Wherever he went they followed – and on the way he taught them, often withdrawing them from the crowds in order to teach them more effectively and personally in private. There are few things more eloquent of Jesus' power with people than this following.

As we have seen in our study of the sermon on the mount, especially the beatitudes, Jesus from the outset made plain the total demands of the kingdom of God, as well as its completely revolutionary nature. But at least to begin with, the twelve must have enjoyed the popularity and excitement generated by the presence of Jesus. A lot happened to them, around them and through them in those opening months. According to the synoptic gospels, the mood turned significantly and irretrievably at a certain moment in their life with Jesus.

The crucial turning-point

In Matthew's account, this crucial time commenced immediately after Peter's confession of Jesus as 'the Christ, the Son of the living God' at Caesarea Philippi (Matt 16:16) – 'From that time', we are told, 'Jesus began to show his disciples that he must go to Jerusalem and suffer many things from the elders and chief priests and scribes, and be killed, and on the third day be raised' (Matt 16:21). Luke seems to have regarded the cardinal moment to have been only slightly later, 'When the days drew near for him to be received up' and 'he set his face to go to Jerusalem' (Luke 9:51). It may turn out to be the same perspective as Matthew, because Luke mentions the same teaching by Jesus to his disciples about suffering and death, *before* stressing his resolutely setting his face towards Jerusalem and the cross (Luke 9:22).

A number of significant details are recorded in all three gospels, as subsequent events then unfolded. They all point to the determination of Jesus to press home the reality of suffering at the heart of discipleship, in spite of the twelve's reluctance and lack of comprehension. It is important to look at these details if we are genuinely to appreciate the way Jesus held those disciples firm in their decision to follow him, even when the route was becoming extremely hazardous and unpleasant. The three evangelists are consistent in their emphasis at this point, though naturally distinctive over specifics. The relevant passages, from which we will take selected incidents, are Matthew 16:21–17:23; Mark 8:31–9:41; Luke 9:18–62.

When Jesus begins to talk about his suffering and death, Peter is the first not merely to object to such a thought but 'to rebuke him, saying, "God forbid, Lord! This shall never happen to you"' (Matt 16:22).

Although Peter's reaction is eminently understandable and most natural, we learn from Jesus' sharp retort precisely how menacing Peter's attitude turned out to be – 'Get behind me, Satan!' (Matt 16:23).[8] The fact that this peremptory command virtually echoes Jesus' words to Satan himself during the temptations in the wilderness compels us to recall the significance of those temptations, to divert Jesus from the way of the cross. Jesus sees in Peter's well-meaning rebuke another direct attempt by Satan to get him off course, away from the cross. Peter – we can legitimately conclude – wanted the power and the glory of God's kingdom without its suffering. Or, at the very least, he could not comprehend a kingdom which had been coming so forcefully in the previous months of ministry being turned on its head and made into a travesty by the elimination of its king.

In completely uncompromising terms, therefore, Jesus makes it plain to Peter that not merely is the path of suffering the only one he can take, but that any stumbling-block placed in his path by Peter (or anyone else) puts the person responsible in direct opposition to God himself. A most significant fact is that Jesus informs Peter that he is 'not on the side of God, but of men' (Matt 16:23) – the phrase literally means 'You are not thinking God's thoughts, but men's thoughts.'

We might have expected Jesus to tell Peter directly that he was working for the enemy of God, as a natural sequel to having been Satan's mouthpiece. The words Jesus *did* use reveal, however, that Peter was manifesting the normal human approach to kingly power, in seeking to divert Jesus from the cross. It is man's way to hold and use power in an aggressive, dominating, impressive fashion. It is not God's way. Satan does all he can to endorse and establish man's way of exercising power – human ideas of power still predominate in the church. Jesus was determined to show an altogether different kind of power. It is extremely telling that, such was the Master's power with this impetuous disciple, even Jesus' sharp confrontation of Peter over this issue did not lead to Peter's reversing his decision to follow behind Jesus. By the gift of God, Peter had clearly recognised Jesus as the Messiah; but he entirely misunderstood what kind of Messiah he was to be – the 'rock' had swiftly become 'a stumbling-block' (the Greek word translated 'hindrance' in Matt 16:23). Gradually disabused of the misconception, Peter slowly, very slowly, learnt God's ways.

Taking up the cross

Jesus immediately moves from the inevitability of his own cross to the inevitability of his disciples' cross – 'If any man would come after [or 'behind'] me, let him deny himself and take up his cross and follow me' (Matt 16:24). He is reiterating what it means to follow him, so that Peter and the other eleven get it straight. He is walking the way of the cross; they too must walk the way of the cross. If they do not walk that way, they are not following him. That means saying goodbye to their own ideas and desires: 'For whoever would save his life will lose it, and whoever loses his life for my sake will find it. For what will it profit a man, if he gains the world and forfeits his life?' (Matt 16:25–26). Peter still shared normal human aspirations for worldly power – to gain the whole world, if possible.

Not long after this Peter revealed how much he was conditioned by such mercenary considerations. He wanted to know what following Jesus would yield, 'Lo, we have left everything and followed you. What then shall we have?' (Matt 19:27). Jesus' answer to that *later* question is summed up in his remark at *this* stage to the disciples: 'the Son of Man is to come with his angels in the glory of his Father, and then he will repay every man for what he has done' (Matt 16:27) – for Peter (and the all disciples) the repayment will be linked to the way he, they and we have followed Jesus in the way which he has walked.

In all three synoptic gospels the next event is the transfiguration of Jesus: 'His face shone like the sun, and his garments became white as light' and Moses and Elijah conversed with him (Matt 17:1–8). Of the twelve disciples only Peter, James and John were present at the time. Peter, presumably wanting to pin down what looked like being a transitory experience, offered to put up three tents on the mountain – 'one for you and one for Moses and one for Elijah' (Matt 17:4). Luke bluntly adds the comment about Peter's remark, 'not knowing what he said' (Luke 9:33). God's own purpose in the remarkable event can be discerned in the voice which proclaimed: 'This is my beloved Son, with whom I am well pleased; listen to him' (Matt 17:5). These words give the same testimony to Jesus as the Son of God that the Father gave at his baptism by John – with the additional command 'listen to him' (cf. Matt 3:17).

Listening to Jesus

The overall impact of the transfiguration was presumably twofold. Firstly, God's testimony to Jesus at this cardinal point in his ministry, with the cross firmly in his vision, would have strengthened him for all that lay ahead. Secondly, the terse order to the three disciples to listen to Jesus (not, like Peter, coming out with arrogant rebukes about Jesus not going to the cross or venturing ignorant irrelevancies like putting up tents on a mountain) underlined the great importance of the teaching which Jesus was now unfolding. Thus Jesus is recommissioned for his ministry as a suffering, serving Messiah, and the disciples are told to pay full attention to all that he is saying. It is therefore important to notice that they listen very obediently to Jesus when, on the way down from the mountain, he tells them not to tell anyone (including the other nine) about the vision (Matt 17:9–13; Luke 9:36). The listening has begun.

In Luke's account of what ensues, Jesus tackles five key themes, and interlaces them with repeated assertions about his imminent death. These themes, as we will see, have a direct bearing on the subject of power. In each case Jesus shows his striking ability to teach his disciples the truth about God's kingdom in the course of daily events: something happens 'on the way' and the disciples show a certain reaction, then Jesus demonstrates his authority by challenging any false assumptions before sharing the proper perspective – the perspective of the kingdom (cf. Luke 9:37–62).

Jesus regarded his teaching at this time to be so important that, according to Mark's account, he took special care to prevent the crowds finding out where he was, so that he could have uninterrupted time with his disciples:

They went on from there and passed through Galilee. And he would not have any one know it; for he was teaching his disciples, saying to them, 'The Son of Man will be delivered into the hands of men, and they will kill him; and when he is killed, after three days he will rise.' But they did not understand the saying, and they were afraid to ask him (Mark 9:30–32).

Facing up to failure

We now come to the five incidents which gave rise to plain teaching about life under the kingly rule of Jesus.

The first had its origins in events which were unfolding in the valley while the three disciples were with Jesus on the mount of transfiguration. A desperate father had brought his only child, an epileptic, to be healed. Because Jesus was not around at the time, he had asked the remaining nine disciples to make his son better, 'but they could not' – or, literally, 'they did not have the power' (Luke 9:40). All three gospels stress the same truth. In Matthew's account (Matt 17:14–21), the father's diagnosis is epilepsy; in Luke's (Luke 9:37–43), it is 'a spirit' which 'seizes', 'convulses' and 'shatters' the boy, forcing him to cry out; in Mark's (Mark 9:14–29), this 'dumb spirit' 'dashes him down', makes him foam at the mouth, grind his teeth and go rigid – with the effect also of throwing him into fire and water. This situation had left the nine powerless: failure stared them in the face, and they were not helped by the mass of spectators and, according to Mark, the presence of some scribes intent on turning it all into a bitter argument (Mark 9:14).

Failure. How as followers of Jesus are we to deal with failure? The nine were concerned enough to ask Jesus immediately – and privately – why they had been unable to cast out the unclean spirit which lay behind the dramatic physical symptoms in the child. Their readiness to ask Jesus this question is very important. Were they free to do so because Peter, their normal spokesman, had not been party to the failure? He would have found it very difficult to face up to such a failure: any suggestion from anyone, particularly from Jesus, that he could not do something normally sparked off a determined effort to do it (see, e.g., John 13:36–38, as well as

his attitude to being told he could not understand now why
Jesus had to wash his feet, John 13:8).

Jesus answers the disciples' question, 'Why could we not
cast it out?' very plainly: 'Because of your little faith' (Matt
17:19–20). It required not just sudden recourse to urgent
prayer but a habit of prayer that expressed unalloyed dependence on God – backed up, if necessary, by fasting (Matt
17:21). Such humble acceptance of our natural powerlessness, such genuine poverty of spirit, could alone provide the
springboard for true faith in a God who can make mountains
move, let alone set a child free from an unclean spirit and its
ravages. There is no way round this self-humbling: we must
deny ourselves, we must say a resolute no to *our* experience,
our resources, *our* abilities. Had the nine disciples slipped
into self-reliance after their successful missionary journey
among 'the lost sheep of the house of Israel' (Matt 10:1–8)?

Dealing with competitiveness

The second theme in Jesus' teaching of his disciples at this
time is competitiveness. 'An argument arose among them as
to which of them was the greatest' (Luke 9:46). This argument, which seems to have been one of many on the same
subject at different stages, was probably occasioned by the
absence of the three on a glorious mountain-top experience
with Jesus, while the other nine languished in public failure in
the valley without Jesus. Who was the greatest? Obviously
Peter, James and John were a privileged trio – to put it mildly.

Jesus went right to the heart of the matter by placing a child
by his side and saying (as he often had to say), 'he who is least
among you all is the one who is great' (Luke 9:48). The word
for 'least' is the superlative form of 'little ones', the phrase he
often used to describe his disciples. The kingdom of God
consists of little ones who accept that they are little, rejoice in
being little, and strive to be as little as possible. The truly
great disciple is the one who lives such a little life that he says
no to himself and yes to others, becoming their servant: 'If
any one would be first, he must be last of all and servant of all'
(Mark 9:35). So it was irrelevant to the matter of significance

in the kingdom that three had been on the mountain while nine had travailed abortively in the valley. Being on the receiving end of glorious experiences has nothing whatsoever to do with greatness before God, nor has failure in ministry. The kingdom of heaven does not operate on such principles. If there is to be any competitiveness among the followers of Jesus, it must be striving to serve one another, not to outstrip one another.

Competitiveness results from the human need to succeed, to produce results, to be recognised and to be in the limelight. When, as Christians, we succumb to these powerful inner drives, we inevitably cause a competitive spirit to come to the surface in those around us. Instead of denying ourselves, we indulge ourselves. We thereby deviate from the way of the cross and subtly encourage very human – and indeed satanic – connotations of power and importance in the life of the church. On a recent visit to one of the provinces of Canada, I spoke (without previous consultation) on this subject in a gathering attended by members of many local churches and denominations. My host told me afterwards that competitiveness was the most common and destructive characteristic in that area – a fact later substantiated independently by others.

This rivalry among his disciples was a constant thorn in the side of Jesus. It was endemic in the church at Corinth (cf. 1 Cor 3:1–15). It is frequently found today among and within large evangelical congregations which strive to be larger, better and more famous than each other. The very size of these congregations often produces an envious attitude among not-so-large churches, an attitude which reveals precisely the same competitive spirit in those churches also. During the last twenty years I have been a member of four congregations with attendances which happen to have been much higher than most in the neighbourhood. Being an Anglican, these four have all been Anglican churches. One of the most difficult obstacles to overcome has been the unholy combination of pride-in-numbers in the local church on the one hand, and envy-at-success in the diocese on the other. Competitiveness is a cancer. Jesus recognised it as completely hostile to the reality of power which he was teaching and demonstrating.

The sectarian spirit

The third theme in Luke's narrative is sectarianism, a fairly modern term to describe an age-old habit among the followers of Jesus (Luke 9:49–50). Mark gives us the fullest account of the incident which revealed this tendency in the disciples:

John said to Jesus, 'Teacher, we saw a man casting out demons in your name, and we forbade him, because he was not following us.' But Jesus said, 'Do not forbid him; for no one who does a mighty work in my name will be able soon after to speak evil of me. For he that is not against us is for us. For truly, I say to you, whoever gives you a cup of water to drink because you bear the name of Christ, will by no means lose his reward' (Mark 9:38–41).

In brief, John was revealing here the common tendency to write off Christian disciples who do not see, talk or do it *our* way. He believed, probably with genuine conviction, that only the twelve were truly following Jesus (it is intriguing to discover how often this word 'follow', which is at the heart of discipleship, seems to occur during these determinative events). John, no doubt endorsed by the eleven, wanted to claim a monopoly for authentic discipleship. He intended to draw a line around the importance and power of the twelve. He saw them not merely as a privileged élite, but as the only ones entitled to determine the true from the false. He had a proprietary and exclusivist approach to the kingdom of God. He would probably – at that time – have denied it, but he saw entrance into the kingdom and membership of the kingdom as privileges to be safeguarded from intruders, entrepreneurs and the like (the 'hirelings' of John 10), rather than as promises to be proclaimed as widely as possible.

At the heart of sectarianism is the desire to control others. This desire leads to splinter-groups breaking off from existing congregations to form their own fellowship. The same desire leads more established congregations to label all such events as wrong, misguided and dangerous. Neither attitude can acknowledge the presence and the activity of God in the other people. Both want to preserve their own position, their own power over people. The way to do that, they assume, is to 'un-church' the others – i.e. to assert that the others have left the mainstream of Christian discipleship and sailed off down a sidewater (which invariably they reckon is heading for disaster). Under the present pope, Pope John Paul 2, the Roman Catholic Church is tending, once again, to take up this sectarian attitude towards all other churches. It stems from their determination to control people and to keep them clearly under their thumb. It is, of course, all too easy to respond to such sectarianism with our own sectarianism, which in this case decides to dismiss not just the Roman Catholic Church but all Roman Catholics from the community of true disciples of Jesus.

The reaction of Jesus to John's sectarianism is fascinating. In Mark's account, it is clear that the key phrase throughout is 'in your name . . . in my name . . . because you bear the name of Christ'. The name of Jesus is the operative principle – not literally the name 'Jesus' but the significance of taking that name as our sign of belonging to Jesus as Lord and Saviour. If a person lives under that name, he is not to be prevented or forbidden from doing so because he does not happen to see other things the way we do. Once a person has submitted himself to Jesus as Lord, he has shown that he is no longer against Jesus (Matt 12:30), but for him (Mark 9:40) – and therefore no longer against his followers ('us' in Mark 9:40, 'you' in Luke 9:50), but right with them. Not to welcome such disciples is to reject Jesus himself.

John did not want to associate himself with this man's ministry at all. Jesus' reply effectively challenged John to set aside his sectarian exclusivity, and to welcome the man as a fellow worker. In other words, it is not adequate simply to accept a man as a brother; we are expected by Jesus to co-operate with him in practical ministry. If we claim to be doing the first while refusing to do the second, we are not letting Jesus deal with our sectarianism in the slightest. In the light of John's attitude towards this independent operator, it is not surprising that Jesus surnamed him and his brother James 'sons of thunder' (Mark 3:17) – a nickname which seems to have been doubly justified in the light of the next incident in Luke's account, as we shall see.

John saw power, including the power of God's kingdom, as something to be preserved at all costs – by erecting a wall around it, by denying it to anybody else except those 'following us', by keeping it to himself and his friends. This was the very antithesis of the attitude of Jesus, who consistently showed that his power was to be given away, shared, poured out for others. His name, the name of Christ the Messiah, should produce in all his followers the freedom to give, not to keep. Mark's addition of the saying about a cup of cold water (Mark 9:41) is, for this reason, entirely apposite. When a follower of Jesus enters into the true nature of his messiahship and its utterly distinctive power, he is then freed to give away anything that he can: it may be only a cup of water, but that will not go unnoticed by Jesus. The important thing, in the eyes of Jesus, is to give, not how impressive or large the gift is. His power sets us free to give.

Racial prejudice

The two 'sons of thunder' hit the jackpot in the fourth incident. They show just how deep and how 'natural' is their antipathy to the way of Jesus. Their problem is as old as Babel and as contemporary as Johannesburg – racial prejudice. Remembering that 'Jews have no dealings with Samaritans' (John 4:9), we read the following narrative:

> When the days drew near for him to be received up, he set his face to go to Jerusalem. And he sent messengers ahead of him, who went and entered a village of the Samaritans, to make ready for him; but the people would not receive him, because his face was set toward Jerusalem. And when his disciples James and John saw it, they said, 'Lord, do you want us to bid fire come down from heaven and consume them?' But he turned and rebuked them, and he said, 'You do not know what manner of spirit you are of; for the Son of man came not to destroy men's lives but to save them.' And they went on to another village (Luke 9:51–56).

Confronted with blatant racial prejudice from the Samaritan villagers, James and John react in kind – not merely with racial prejudice but with hearts bent on reprisal. More than that, they presume to call down fire from heaven to wreak their vengeance – thus betraying their own conception of what the kingdom of God is like. They had learnt very little about Jesus and power. Not only did they entirely misunderstand the nature of God's power, they imagined that any use of that power was a legitimate means to securing what they fondly imagined to be God's purposes – and the wishes of Jesus.

In rebuking them for their reactions, Jesus makes at least four important points, explicitly or implicitly, about life in the kingdom of God. First, retaliation is out: he made that plain in the sermon on the mount – 'Do not resist one who is evil. But if any one strikes you on the right cheek, turn to him the other also' (Matt 5:39). Secondly, racial prejudice is equally hostile to the life of God's kingdom: and we cannot reply to such prejudice in others with similar attitudes and behaviour. Thirdly, God does not use his power to consume those who behave in a way which contradicts his kingdom. Fourthly, whenever we react in any of the previous three ways, we betray the source of our behaviour to lie with Satan, not with Jesus.

Jesus wanted James and John to appreciate how deeply their anti-Christian attitudes resided in their inner beings. They were revealing what lay in their hearts: 'For out of the abundance of the heart the mouth speaks . . . what comes out of the mouth proceeds from the heart, and this defiles a man' (Matt 12:34; 15:18). Their misconceptions about the kingdom of God and what it meant to follow Jesus were due not simply to intellectual confusion or mental blocks but to inner perversity. Jesus' power with his disciples lay in his consistent determination to go right to the heart of both the matter and the man. For Jesus the kingdom of God came first; it had to be the same for all those who wanted to follow him.

With a whole heart

This wholeheartedness is the theme of the fifth and last incident, or series of incidents, in this particular part of Luke's gospel (Luke 9:57–62). The theme is clearly what it means to 'follow' Jesus. The actual word comes three times, twice expressing the determination of would-be disciples ('I will follow you . . .', Luke 9:57, 61) and once on the lips of Jesus, echoing his initial and continuous call to the twelve ('Follow me', Luke 9:59). Jesus focuses attention on what following him means in terms of the kingdom of God: 'No one who puts his hand to the plough and looks back is fit for the kingdom of God' (Luke 9:62). He, Jesus, the king of the kingdom, must come *first* in each disciple's life: we must 'seek *first* his kingdom and his righteousness' (Matt 6:33). He stresses this priority in response to two potential followers who have said: 'Lord, let me *first* go and bury my father . . . let me *first* say farewell to those at my home' (Luke 9:59, 61).

The secret of power in the kingdom of God is to put Jesus first. The secret of Jesus' power with people is that he demanded that they thus put him first – and then he demonstrated by his own life that his first priority was to be a servant of all, to give himself away, to walk the way of the cross. It is a strange power when the king of the kingdom has nowhere to lay his head (Luke 9:58). All the attitudes he confronted in his disciples were a contradiction of the kingdom of God and the nature of true power: he compelled his followers to face up to failure, competitiveness, sectarianism and racial prejudice – to face up to them as they lay deep within their inner hearts, and to deal with them in ways consistent with the kingdom of God. They were tempted to see discipleship in terms of getting, grabbing, keeping, snatching, controlling and retaliating. He saw it – and lived it out – in terms of giving, serving, welcoming, forgiving.

5 WHO CARES FOR THE DOWNTRODDEN? – POWER AND THE POWERLESS

The Palestine into which Jesus was born was reeling under the impact of over thirty years under Herod the Great. He had embarked on massive spending at home and abroad, undertaking ambitious schemes which he financed with heavy taxation. These taxes he collected ruthlessly by means of 'publicans' (or tax collectors) in each town and in Jerusalem. The fact that the taxes were exorbitant and were being used to fuel his own ambitions served only to exacerbate the dishonesty of the tax collectors in the eyes of the people. A privileged few were lining their own pockets at the expense of the impoverished many.

By the time Herod the Great died, soon after the birth of Jesus, the whole country had been reduced to poverty. The people were demoralised. Any sense of morality had been seriously weakened. They were resigned to misfortune. The same approach to government characterised Herod's successor, Archelaus. From AD 6 Herod Agrippa I held the reins of government; taxes remained cripplingly high, but he avoided the same popular hatred by mounting up a huge national debt. One of the spin-offs of the whole situation was widespread venality among officials, of the kind which is so common in many Third World countries in similar economic conditions today.

In the country areas of Palestine, where an agrarian economy was the order of the day, very few people had regular employment. A system of day labourers was the norm and the situation became extremely serious if there was no work, particularly in the event of a poor harvest and, worst of all, famine. The net result of these circumstances was that, even at the best of times, a large section of the population was dependent on charity of various kinds.

This was especially true in Jerusalem. Its location meant that there was no supply of raw materials for light industry. Being on high ground, it had a very poor and inadequate water supply. It was most unsuitably located for trade and commerce. The entire life of Jerusalem revolved around the temple. During the last twenty years of the first century BC and the first sixty years of the first century AD, when the temple was being rebuilt in all its magnificence, probably one-third of the city's workforce was employed on the building-works. In addition, the different trades involved in the cultus – e.g. bakers, weavers, goldsmiths, barbers – accounted for a significant proportion of those employed. There was, also, a high proportion of trade involved in the commercial aspect of temple life – luxury goods, like gold, alabaster, marble and cedarwood, oil, incense, wine and grain; animals of different kinds for sacrifices; costly items like clothing and jewellery. We also ought to recognise the spasmodic and seasonal employment (e.g. in providing accommodation and food) created by the three major religious festivals each year, when the number of visiting pilgrims increased the city population from 25,000 to about 120,000. People who owned their own businesses did particularly well out of this pattern of employment in first-century Judea.

The perpetual poor

Overall, however, there was a large majority of extremely poor and hopeless people. The gulf between these multitudes and the priestly aristocracy which surrounded the court of the Herods was vast. Among the impoverished masses there was a strident minority of beggars. Not least because almsgiving in the holy city had particular religious merit, Jerusalem became a focus for begging. You could never tell an authentic beggar from a charlatan. People often pretended to be dumb, deaf, blind, lame or otherwise handicapped. Outside the city gates the lepers begged for alms. Cripples were only allowed limited access to the temple. In addition, you could find an indeterminate number of scroungers, who simply hung around at special celebrations such as weddings or bar mitzvahs and sponged off the host families. Even the ordinary cost of living was inflated in the city, as distinct from the country areas, because of the usual 'rip-offs' made by profiteers. When you add to all these factors the presence of a considerable number of slaves in Jerusalem, you have an accurate picture of a country weighed down with massive exploitation, widespread unemployment, inflated prices, and little or no prospect of improvement – and all these things in a religion-dominated society and under the heel of a ruthless army of hated foreigners. It is not surprising that Jesus himself said on one occasion: 'The poor you always have with you' (John 12:8).

'He has anointed me to preach good news to the poor' (Luke 4:18) – that was how Jesus described his ministry in the power of the Spirit at the outset. The passage from Isaiah, which he was thereby claiming to be fulfilled in himself, spoke of the captives, the blind and the oppressed as being the principal beneficiaries. These were the poor whom Jesus proceeded to draw with his good news. Blind eyes were literally opened, but we do not read of any prisons being emptied of their captives. Many people oppressed in all kinds of ways – by leprosy, evil spirits, incurable illness, congenital conditions, epilepsy – were set at liberty; but the oppression of occupation forces was not removed.

It is impossible, therefore, to be simplistic about the ministry of Jesus to the poor. The good news can never, on the evidence of the New Testament, be restricted to the inauguration of a new social order in which equality and justice rule. If that had been the ultimate or the major objective of Jesus, we would presumably have seen a far more explicit confrontation of those in authority, a far more obvious use of power to bring in the righteousness of God. What we have gathered so far about both the active power in Jesus and his way of exercising it makes it clear that in the kingdom of God which Jesus was establishing it is the power to serve and to give which prevails, not the power either to hold on to what we already have or to snatch at what we feel we ought to have.

The challenge of the gospel

The gospel of the kingdom of God is therefore a direct challenge both to the rapacity of the rich and to the covetousness of the poor. What Jesus looked for in potential citizens of the kingdom was childlike dependence on God, true poverty of spirit, and the eagerness to say no to oneself and yes to serving others. Then as now, he was more likely to find those qualities in the helpless rather than in the achiever, in the oppressed rather than in the oppressor, in the sick and starving rather than in the hale and hearty, in the poor rather than in the rich, in the powerless rather than the powerful. On this basis, urban priority areas in the UK (for example) become potential arenas in which the kingdom of God will find the most fertile ground.

The Chilean writer Segundo Galilea has an eloquent modern parable to explain this 'bias to the poor' in the message and ministry of Jesus.

We are in a miserable little village of the Andes. The vast majority of its people are very poor. There are no health facilities here, no hospital, no medicines, no doctors or nurses. Neither have these poor the money to travel to the city for treatment if they fall ill. So they suffer a great deal from their illnesses, and they die prematurely. In the same village, as often happens, there is also a group of families in more comfortable circumstances. These latter can afford to journey to the city to be looked after, and can afford to purchase medicines. Unlike their fellow villagers, they do not live in deprivation.

One day a clinic is set up in the village. It is well staffed and well equipped. Now the people can be treated for their diseases right in their village. Furthermore the clinic is free. It offers its services and its medicines gratis.

Now comes the day of the formal opening. A priest is asked to bless the new facility. He says – this minister of Christ: 'You are the happy ones today, you, the poor of this village. For this clinic is yours. It belongs to you.'

At first glance it may seem that the priest's assertion is

not precisely accurate. Actually the clinic is for everyone, is it not? It is free for everyone – everyone in the village, both the poor and the comfortable. So why does the priest mention only the poor?

For a very good reason. It is the poor who have most reason to rejoice, most reason to be 'happy' about the clinic. For the poor, more than for those of the village in more comfortable circumstances, the clinic is the fulfill-ment of an ancient promise. It is 'good news'. It is a great source of hope. True, the clinic is not for them alone. It is for rich and poor alike. *But its primary beneficiaries are the poor*.

. . . The mere fact of [the clinic's] existence is no guaran-tee of the health of the poor or anyone else. People must take advantage of the clinic. They must avail themselves of its services, submit to treatment. They must take their medicine. Similarly, the poor must follow Jesus and his teachings in order to possess their kingdom.[1]

In this helpful way Segundo Galilea explains the Lucan version of the first beatitude: 'Blessed [or 'happy'] are you poor, because yours is the kingdom of God' (Luke 6:20). The literally and materially impoverished were – and are – far more ready to acknowledge their spiritual poverty, and there-fore to turn to the Lord. This always has proved to be the case, from the ministry of Jesus onwards: 'Those who are well have no need of physician, but those who are sick.' To those who, in the secrecy of their private thoughts or in open scepticism, pour scorn on a gospel which offers such a crutch to needy people, Jesus himself replies, 'Go and learn what this means, "I desire mercy, and not sacrifice." For I came not to call the righteous, but sinners' (Matt 9:12–13).

At the same time we must note that these words about 'those who are sick' and 'sinners' were spoken by Jesus not to explain his association with the poor but when he was criti-cised by the Pharisees for eating and drinking with tax col-lectors and prostitutes, neither of whom would have been economically poor. A brief overview of the ministry of Jesus to the powerless will substantiate this perspective. We will also, I believe, be able to hold the more dramatic and humanly impressive side of his ministry in balance. Frequently today we find the miracles, especially of healing and exorcism, being held up as an essential aspect of his ministry, but in a way which fails to place them in the context of his character, teaching and example. Having done our homework on these other matters in the previous chapters of this book, we are in a better position to see how the signs and wonders express – in both point and counterpoint – the servant aspects of Jesus' messiahship.

Helping the helpless

It is impossible, when reading through any one of the gospels, not to be impressed by the sheer magnetism of Jesus with the vast crowds which flocked after him. On numerous occasions Matthew tells us that 'great crowds' followed him. On virtually every occasion he ministered to those in need, usually 'those afflicted with various diseases and pains, demoniacs, epileptics, and paralytics' (Matt 4:24). At other times the evangelists highlight his ministry to particular individuals who were drawn to him by his magnetic deeds, words and personality. Whether they suffered from leprosy or blindness, internal haemorrhaging or a common fever, a withered hand or a crooked back – he healed them. Of the various words used to describe the impact of these many sicknesses and diseases on people, the most common are ones like 'afflicted', 'distressed', 'troubled', 'suffered', 'oppressed'. It is striking how often the emphasis falls on this aspect of their condition.

We can see already that Jesus was willing to help those who were helpless to do anything about their condition. In some cases they had tried everything and everybody else; in other cases the condition was incurable or untouchable for medical or religious reasons, or both. The people concerned – or their friends and relatives – had nowhere to turn but to Jesus. They were without resources and they readily acknowledged the fact: their poverty in spirit may have been forced upon them, but it was no less real and genuine for that.

When we take another look at the words used by the evangelists to describe the actual ministry of Jesus in such

situations, another intriguing fact emerges. The Greek lan-
gauge has a number of words for 'heal', three of which are
used in the synoptic gospels of the healing ministry of Jesus.
Sozo is used twice and *iaomai* sixteen times, but a third word,
therapeuo – which has several obvious derivatives in modern
English – is far and away the most common. Matthew, Mark
and Luke all use it more frequently than either of the other
two words – in fact a total of thirty-two occasions, or twice as
much as the second alternative. The significance of this option
is that the word has the primary meaning of 'be a servant' or
'serve'. The evangelists presumably preferred the nuance of
this word because it highlighted the servant nature of Jesus'
healing ministry. His power in healing was not to show power
over people, but to release them for greater effectiveness – as
a servant by his actions seeks to enable his master to be better
equipped for his daily life.

Healing as a servant ministry

To stress healing as a servant ministry is most necessary in
many Christian circles today. The power which came from
Jesus to those suffering through sickness or demonic activity
was the power to come alongside and support, not to manipulate and to dominate. He deliberately took steps to break any
dependency in the case of the Gadarene demoniac, who
wanted to follow Jesus and continue with him *ad infinitum*.
Jesus 'refused, and said to him, "Go home to your friends,
and tell them how much the Lord has done for you, and how
he has had mercy on you"' (Mark 5:19).

This factor is emphasised when we recognise how many
miracles of healing were performed either in the context of
confrontation with the religious hierarchy or in direct protest
against their rigid domination of ordinary people by legalistic
requirements – for example, in connection with the sabbath.
Jesus insisted, in the light of this overbearing oppression of
ordinary people by those in religious power, that he was Lord
of the sabbath, that the sabbath was made for man and not
vice versa, and that it is totally in line with God's will to cure
and save life on the sabbath, not to kill and destroy (see Matt
12:1–14).

Immediately before this particular clash with the Pharisees, Jesus had issued his glorious invitation to everyone who was weary and heavy-laden: 'Come to me . . . and I will give you rest' (Matt 11:28). We note both the context in which Matthew places this invitation, and Jesus' later reference to the heavy burdens placed on the people by the Pharisees (Matt 23:4). These two factors together point to Jesus' keen awareness of the powerlessness of ordinary people when it was a question of escaping from underneath these grinding minutiae of legal obligations. The wider implications of Jesus' approach to those with religious power will be examined in a later chapter. Suffice it to say that the servant ministry of Jesus is extremely clear in this particular setting of religious oppression. The power exercised by Jesus was in complete contrast to the power exercised by the scribes and Pharisees.

In general, we can see a frequent theme running like a golden thread through the healing ministry of Jesus: he was available to serve those who, for whatever reason, were helpless in the face of social, religious, physical or psychological pressures arising either from their condition or from their circumstances, or from both. This thread is not always present, let alone obvious: but we can think of the following examples – lepers ostracised from normal human society and all public religious observance (Mark 1:40–45); the servant of a Roman centurion, doubly handicapped by his servant status and by his employment in a Roman's household (Matt 8:5–13); the Gadarene demoniac(s) expelled from the local community and forced to live chained up in tombs (Matt 8:28–34; Mark 5:1–20); a paralytic completely unable to move himself (Luke 5:17–26); a woman suffering from continual internal bleeding, given up – and impoverished – by doctors and ceremonially unclean (Luke 8:42b–48); blind men reduced to begging for subsistence (Matt 20:29–34); a Canaanite woman with a demonised daughter, regarded by Jews as one of 'the dogs' (Mark 7:24–30).

Such captives, blind men and oppressed people heard and rejoiced to receive the good news that was for both poor and rich, for all who were ready to see in their current situation evidence of their need for God. Some who came to Jesus and found such salvation were by no stretch of the imagination literally poor – for example, Jairus, the centurion and Zacchaeus would all have been comfortably off – but they were powerless to help themselves.

Continuing this overview of Jesus' ministry to the powerless, three principles seem to stand out as pointers to the power he manifested – he was a man under authority; he was a man moved with compassion; he was a man who encouraged others to have faith in God. It will be valuable to look at each principle in some detail.

A man under authority

First, Jesus was a man under authority. Initially the evangelists note that he was a man *with* authority, especially in his teaching and most of all in his ministry with those who were demonised. But not long after, according to Matthew and Luke, the true secret of his authority is discerned by a foreigner – by the Roman centurion whose servant was desperately ill at home (Matt 8:5–13). Not reckoning himself worthy to have Jesus actually come under his roof, he requests Jesus simply to 'say the word, and my servant will be healed' (Matt 8:8). In giving a simple explanation for his conviction that this authoritative command from Jesus would bring healing, he says, 'I myself am a man under authority' (Matt 8:9 NIV). The centurion knew that Jesus possessed authority because he was living under a higher authority. That was how it worked in the Roman army – in any army: he could give authoritative commands, and his men would obey instantly, but only because he himself was under the authority of his senior officers, and ultimately of Tiberius Caesar himself.

We cannot tell, of course, how much the Roman centurion understood about Jesus' submission to his Father: probably only a little, and that by instinct. But he was showing an understanding of the secret of Jesus' power which was quite remarkable – as Jesus himself was the first to testify: 'Truly, I say to you, not even in Israel have I found such faith' (Matt 8:10). We will return to the theme of faith later; at this stage it is important to stay with the insight expressed by the centurion, that Jesus had authority because he was under authority.

This truth lies at the heart of John's distinctive expression of the relationship between Jesus and his Father. Consider the following words of Jesus, as recorded in John's gospel:

> Truly, truly, I say to you, the Son can do nothing of his own accord, but only what he sees the Father doing; for whatever he does, that the Son does likewise. For the Father loves the Son, and shows him all that he himself is doing . . . I can do nothing on my own authority . . . I seek not my own will but the will of him who sent me . . . The works which the Father has granted me to accomplish, these very works which I am doing, bear me witness that the Father has sent me (John 5:19–20, 30, 36).

> I do nothing on my own authority but speak thus as the Father taught me. And he who sent me is with me; he has not left me alone, for I always do what is pleasing to him . . . I speak of what I have seen with my Father . . . I have not spoken on my own authority; the Father who sent me has himself given me commandment what to say and what to speak . . . What I say, therefore, I say as the Father has bidden me (John 8:28–29, 38; 12:49–50).

> The words that I say to you I do not speak on my own authority; but the Father who dwells in me does his works . . . I do as the Father has commanded me, so that the world may know that I love the Father . . . When the Spirit of truth comes, he will guide you into all the truth; for he will not speak on his own authority, but whatever he hears he will speak . . . he will take what is mine and declare it to you. All that the Father has is mine; therefore I said that he will take what is mine and declare it to you (John 14:10, 31; 16:13–15).

The secret of Jesus' power and authority lay in his total submission to the Father's will, word, ways and works. Because he was thus held firm in and by his Father's love, God was able to trust him with power which in anyone else's hands would have been abused and therefore lethal. No wonder Satan from the outset tried to undermine Jesus' relationship

of submission and obedience to the Father. The devil longed
for Jesus, just once, to exercise his power on his own authority, not under the authority of the Father. In wanting Jesus
to behave like that, he was trying to make Jesus like himself.
He had snatched at equality with God; he had succeeded in
tempting Adam and Eve into snatching at equality with God;
he had only to force the Son of God to snatch at equality with
God and he had won all he ever wanted. But Jesus steadily
refused to snatch at anything, because hc knew that being
equal with God (indeed, actually *being* God) does not consist
in snatching at anything, but rather in serving and giving. He
remained a man under authority throughout his earthly life,
especially through his suffering and death.

Casting out demons

It is significant that Jesus was at his most direct and peremptory with Satan both in the wilderness, when he tried to move
Jesus out of his submission to the authority of the Father, and
in his public ministry, when demons were wreaking their
destructive and possessive power before his very eyes. As the
evangelists themselves note, the authority of Jesus is never
more obvious than in such confrontation with the minions of
Satan. Presumably this is because the spiritual issues of good
and evil are most clearly delineated in such circumstances –
that is, with Jesus acting under God's authority to set free and
to make whole, and the demons acting in defiance of God's
authority to enslave and destroy. It is not surprising, therefore, that it is in the context of such ministry by Jesus that he
makes his plainest statement about discipleship: 'He who is
not with me is against me, and he who does not gather with me
scatters' (Luke 11:14–26, esp. 23). There are no grey areas in
this conflict, no such thing as no-man's-land, no convenient
fence on which we can assume either neutrality or the luxury
of being a 'don't know'.

The different kinds of power and attitudes to power in Jesus
and in Satan are vividly expressed in the two words translated
'gathers' and 'scatters'. The first word, describing what is
characteristic of the kingdom of God, literally means 'brings

together'. The power of Jesus is integrative, makes whole, unites, mends, heals, restores, liberates. The second word, describing what is characteristic of the kingdom of Satan, literally means 'chases in all directions' and is used of a wolf scattering sheep in the teaching about Jesus as the good shepherd (John 10:12). Both gathering and scattering are words used of sheep; Jesus insists that we are either gathering the sheep together or, by default, involved in scattering them. A similar contrast between two diametrically opposed kinds of power is drawn by Jesus in John 10 between on the one hand the shepherd, who delights to feed and protect and lead the sheep, and on the other both the hireling, who does not care at all for the sheep, and the thief, who comes 'only to steal and kill and destroy' (John 10:10). Jesus brings life; Satan dispenses destruction and death.

In his own mission of destroying (or reversing) 'the works of the devil' (1 John 3:8), Jesus (according to John) died in order 'to gather into one the children of God who are scattered abroad' (John 11:52). The word for 'scatter' is, in fact, the word from which we get 'scorpion'. It is therefore interesting to notice that Jesus gave his disciples 'authority to tread upon serpents and scorpions, and over all the power of the enemy. (Luke 10:19). At the same time, he urged them not to focus on the fact that the demons are under their authority, but to 'rejoice that your names are written in heaven' (Luke 10:20) – i.e. that Jesus is Lord and that he has saved them for eternity. This remained true even at the darkest hour of his life, 'the hour . . . of darkness' (Luke 22:53), when Satan's desperate final fling resulted in the shepherd being struck and the sheep being scattered (Matt 26:31; cf. Zech 13:7), 'every man to his home' (John 16:32) as the disciples one by one fell away from him.

Moving, thus, under the authority of his heavenly Father, Jesus deliberately confronted Satan and his demons head-on in his ministry. He rebuked the demons (Luke 9:42); he cast them out (Matt 8:16); he would not permit them to speak (Mark 1:25); he strictly ordered them not to make him known (Luke 4:41); he commanded them to come out (Luke 4:35); he forbade them to enter the person again (Mark 9:25). Here was sovereign power and total authority, making it plain that

Jesus was stronger than the strong man, even when that strong man, 'with all his weapons ready', is guarding his own palace and 'all his belongings are safe' (Luke 11:21 GNB). Initially in the power struggle in the wilderness, consistently throughout his public ministry, supremely through his death and resurrection, and ultimately when the last enemy – death itself – will be eliminated, Jesus through his submission to the Father took away the armour in which Satan had trusted, notably his ability to deceive mankind about God's character and kingdom. In Jesus, 'a man under authority' (Matt 8:9), the nature and the source of true power were perfectly revealed.

A man of compassion

The second principle at the heart of Jesus' ministry to the powerless was his compassion. This is a necessary corollary to his being a man under authority, a characteristic which on its own could produce a clinical efficiency and a ruthless obedience to a higher power without any warmth or sensitivity. We need think only of some of the ugliest crimes committed by men like Joseph Mengele or Adolf Eichmann, acting under the authority of Hitler. Submission to God and compassion for people, however, is an extremely powerful and attractive combination. Jesus was 'filled with compassion'. The way the evangelists use the phrase indicates that this compassion was the driving impetus behind his ministry to the powerless.

For example, it was compassion which moved him to heal a leper; to bring back to life the widow of Nain's son; to commission his disciples to preach the kingdom of God to the harassed and helpless multitudes, with power to heal and cast out demons; to teach the word of God to those hungry for spiritual nourishment; to provide food for the starving; to bring healing to crowds of sick people; to give sight to the blind (Mark 1:41; Luke 7:13; Matt 9:36–10:1; Mark 6:34; Matt 15:32; 14:14; 20:34). This panorama of human need moved Jesus deeply in his guts (the root meaning of the Greek word for compassion) and was the springboard for showing his power to the powerless.

We must, at this stage, remind ourselves that the religious perspective of the Pharisees treated sickness as the result of personal sin. As a direct consequence, the sick in the time of Jesus were pushed to the margins of society. There are few more deliberately confrontational aspects of Jesus' ministry than his compassionate healing of the sick. On at least one specific occasion he refused to countenance any such connection between a person's physical condition and the sin of either the individual or his parents (John 9:1–12).

This compassion, which is the driving characteristic of God himself ('the Lord is full of compassion and gracious', Ps 103:8; cf. 145:8 RV), is the direct antithesis of the driving force behind Satan's power – hatred and greed. The compassion of Jesus led him to give himself away, to say No to himself, to lay down his life, to take up his cross, and to give his life as a ransom for many.

One of the passages in which the general healing ministry of Jesus is described also contains an important perspective on his compassion. In particular, it gives suggestive guidelines for any such ministry today. Matthew quotes the prophet Isaiah:

> Behold, my servant whom I have chosen,
>> my beloved with whom my soul is well pleased.
> I will put my Spirit upon him,
>> and he shall proclaim justice to the Gentiles.
> He will not wrangle or cry aloud,
>> nor will any one hear his voice in the streets;
> he will not break a bruised reed
>> or quench a smouldering wick,
> till he brings justice to victory;
>> and in his name will the Gentiles hope.
>
> (Matt 12:18–21; cf. Isa 42:1–4)

The ministry of Jesus to the powerless was neither strident nor noisy. He was concerned, if anything, to keep it in low profile and to enable the timid, battered and bruised folk to make their way to him. If he detected merely the flicker of faith, he carefully fanned it into a flame. When the public gaze was too glaring for a wounded spirit, he would not hesitate to put everyone – including his disciples – outside the room. This tender sensitivity is seen particularly in the way he ministers as a servant to children who are desperately ill.

It is very easy, as ministers of Jesus, not to be fired with the same compassion, but rather to see and treat the powerless as material for miracles. This opportunism represents a classic sell-out to Satan, who is constantly tempting us to exercise power in a selfish, snatching way. If there is the slightest whiff of either sensationalism or pride or impatience with 'difficult cases', we ought to be re-examining our motives and, indeed, our whole ministry. Do we want to see God's power at work because our hearts ache with the pain and distress of those whose lives are so harassed and helpless? Or is success in such a ministry necessary for our own image, prosperity or even identity?

A man who emphasised faith

The third principle at work in the ministry of Jesus to the powerless was the way he encouraged them to show faith in God. In general, this faith was clearly evident in the trouble taken by the people of every city, town and village to come to him with their needs. The problem for Jesus was not persuading the people to come, but giving himself space in which to minister effectively – especially to nurture his own relationship of trust and submission towards his Father. Jesus normally interpreted the people's eagerness to come to him with their needs as indicative of true faith. He stressed in his teaching that he was concerned to find faith only as large as 'a grain of mustard seed' (Matt 17:20; Luke 17:6). Given that, mountains could be moved.

In fact, Jesus actually likened the kingdom of God as a whole to a grain of mustard seed 'which when sown upon the ground, is the smallest of all the seeds on earth; yet when it is sown it grows up and becomes the greatest of all shrubs, and puts forth large branches, so that the birds of the air can make nests in its shade' (Mark 4:30–32). Faith, like submission and compassion, is of the very essence of God's kingdom and therefore of true power.

When in a narrative describing the power of Jesus at work in someone powerless to help himself the evangelists specifically mention faith, inevitably the reason is to highlight the absence of faith or to ensure that bystanders (or readers of the gospel) understand the importance of faith or to elicit deeper faith (perhaps its public confession) in the person involved. For example, we have the picture of unbelief 'in his own country': the result being that 'he did not do many mighty works there, because of their unbelief' (Matt 13:58). Alternatively, the woman with internal bleeding who touched the fringe of Jesus' cloak in the crowds was brought out from her secrecy for her own sake *and* for the benefit of the others – so that everyone (the woman, the crowds and the disciples) could hear the declaration of Jesus, 'Daughter, your faith has made you well; go in peace, and be healed of your disease' (Mark 5:34).

Perhaps the clearest example of Jesus drawing out and deepening the minuscule faith of a person in great need is in dealing with the father of the demonised boy, whose faith must have been severely eroded by the powerlessness of the nine disciples, as well as by the cynical comments of the local scribes (Mark 9:14–29). When the man cries out in desperation to Jesus, 'If you can do anything, have pity (or 'compassion') on us and help us', Jesus reacts with remarkable directness: 'If *you* can! All things are possible to him who believes.' The man's response has become the classic statement of countless people down the centuries, 'I believe; help my unbelief!' (Mark 9:22–24). Jesus does precisely that and ministers in power to the child – the very best way of helping unbelief. Incidentally, the story is valuable, also, because of the way the father's initial plea to Jesus introduces the three elements in 'kingdom-power' now under examination – submission, compassion and faith.

Not infrequently, especially in Matthew, the importance of faith is underlined by its shining presence in the most unlikely people. For example, Jesus 'marvelled' at the expectancy he found in the Roman centurion, 'Truly, I say to you, with no one in Israel have I found such faith . . . Go; be it done for you as you have believed' (Matt 8:10 (RSV margin), 13). Again, in his striking encounter with a Canaanite woman near

Tyre and Sidon, Jesus responded eventually to her insistent demands and sharp repartee with the words, 'O woman, great is your faith! Be it done for you as you desire' (Matt 15:28). The same unexpected faith is found in two blind men, whom Jesus challenges, 'Do you believe that I am able to do this?' When they reply, 'Yes, Lord,' he touches their eyes and says, 'According to your faith be it done to you' (Matt 9:28–29).

When people who were powerless to do anything about their situation showed mustard-seed faith, Jesus ministered in power to their needs. By stressing the triggering impact of even tiny faith, he increased people's capacity for faith. By firmly insisting that a person who had been healed confess it openly, he enabled others to appreciate the importance of faith. By highlighting the presence of exceptional faith in the most unexpected people, he removed any notion that God had any favourites, and encouraged even the most despised and rejected to develop faith.

Jesus the author of faith

Jesus planted faith, nurtured faith, responded to faith. He was 'the author . . . of . . . faith' (Heb 12:2 NIV). We do not catch a whiff of that judgmental and rejecting attitude, prevalent today in many Christian circles, which blames the non-occurrence of healing on the absent or inadequate faith of those who genuinely do believe that Jesus can heal them – even if that faith is only the size of a grain of mustard seed. Jesus was prevented from working 'many mighty works' in Nazareth not because he did not find enough faith but 'because of their unbelief' (Matt 13:58). There is a world of difference between the two. Unbelief is not merely the absence of faith, it is the refusal to believe. Faith is not to be measured arithmetically – a particular failing of the Westerner's preoccupation with quantity and results. Jesus looked for faith *in God* – its content, not its volume.

For many people, both in the time of Jesus and today, the root cause of unbelief is an entrenched fatalism. They do not believe in the power and the love of God; they simply adopt an attitude of despair and a sense of inevitability. They do not hope for any change for the better.

Jesus was able to spread faith in God among such people. He initiated faith so powerful that it spread from one person to the next. 'Wherever the general atmosphere of fatalism had been replaced by an atmosphere of faith, the impossible began to happen'[2] – what we call 'miracles'.

Doubt can exist alongside faith, and often does: when Peter began to walk on the water at the bidding of Jesus, he was showing faith (Matt 14:28–33). Once he started to look at the winds and the waves, he began to sink. Jesus immediately stretched out his hand and caught him. He did not tell Peter that his doubting demonstrated that he did not have faith. He said to him, 'O man of *little* faith, why did you doubt?' Peter's faith, though little enough, was genuine and valid in the eyes of Jesus; but he allowed his eyes to be taken off the Lord, and doubt entered. When Jesus told him to walk towards him on the water, Peter did not show unbelief but faith. When fear crept – or rushed – in, doubt took over and he began to sink. The way we move from fear to faith is to look to Jesus. Peter had done precisely that a moment before, when he was terrified at seeing Jesus walking towards them on the sea. In his fear he said: 'Lord, if it is you, bid me come to you on the water.' Faith then took over – momentarily he walked on the water.

To summarise this important principle: Jesus was not looking for faith before he would bring power to the powerless, he was actively involved in planting and nourishing faith. He did not wait until such people developed great faith; he moved in power to minister to those with mustard-seed faith. If people took offence at him or his message, as at Nazareth, he could not and did not operate in the same way. It is not hard to see the bond between this and his compassion for the powerless on the one hand, and his submission to the Father on the other.

The injunction to silence

Before ending this study of Jesus' power among the powerless, one further subject needs to be mentioned. We cannot help but notice that Jesus often insisted that silence should be maintained about his mighty works and his identity as the Messiah. Certain individuals to whom he brought healing were given this injunction (Mark 1:44; 5:43; 7:36; Matt 9:30; 12:16). When his disciples reached full conviction about his being the Messiah, they were told to keep quiet about it (Mark 8:30). Demons were prevented from talking about him, because they knew who he was (Luke 4:41). What is the link between these three very different groups?

Leaving on one side the lengthy and complex theological debate about 'the messianic secret',[3] we can appreciate the keen desire of Jesus to prevent the people as a whole from misinterpreting the nature of his messiahship. Satan, after all, had concentrated his major assault in the wilderness on this target. He did not change his aim, only his tactics, during the next three years. He used every weapon at his disposal to break Jesus' resolve to exercise his power in a serving, giving, sacrificing way. Jesus was fully aware of these tactics and took steady measures to nullify them.

With his disciples and with the demons he was successful, but some individuals were so full of their healing or cleansing that they chose deliberately to disobey Jesus. Disobedience among those on a spiritual 'high' has always made the mission of Jesus far more difficult. Instead of being helpless and powerless, we receive new power by the goodness and grace of God. We become presumptuous in our new freedom and we use the power for our own purposes and in accordance with our own ideas of what is best for God. Jesus was acutely aware of the dangers involved in his signs and wonders. His injunctions to silence are to 'show that Jesus is not presenting himself as a mere wonder-worker . . . who can be pressured into messiahship by crowds whose messianic views are materialistic and political . . . he came to die, not to trounce the Romans'.[4]

An accurate perspective on this aspect of Jesus and power must therefore include such a dissuader from any tendency to exploit or make capital out of the resources of the kingdom of God. Jesus made them fully available as he fully received them from his Father – under authority, out of compassion, and encouraging faith, but never allowing friends, camp followers or foes to divert him from the way of the cross.

6 THE POSSESSED – THE POWER OF MONEY

The American economist J. K. Galbraith has written, 'Those with wealth usually feel that their views on politics, economics and personal behaviour are meant to be taken seriously *because* of their wealth.'[1]

Money exercises immense power over everyone, even or especially over those who have money. It is generally stated by Christians that, in itself, money is morally neutral. Paul states, it is pointed out, that 'love of money is the root of all evils' (1 Tim 6:10), not money *per se*. And, with this distinction, comes further relaxation into a false sense of security about our ability to resist the power of money; not, of course, that the distinction is wrongly drawn, but that money's immense, pervasive and deceptive power is not properly discerned. Jesus, in his teaching and lifestyle, did not make this mistake.

Jacques Ellul, whose recently translated and republished book *Money and Power* contains much incisive material on this subject, has pointed out a strange paradox in the Old Testament's teaching on money. The Old Testament invariably presents wealth as a blessing, willed by God and pleasing to him: but the wealthy are almost always judged and condemned. Ellul pre-empts objections to this summary by tackling three examples of wealthy men in the Old Testament whose characters do not indicate divine disapproval – Abraham, Job and Solomon. In each case, he argues, God asked them the same question in different ways: Whom do you love? When God had established in each man that he loved God, not his wealth, he entrusted to them material wealth.

Ellul maintains that none of the three is justified in being rich because he gained his wealth fairly or used it well – 'They are justified because of their relationship with God.'[2] He stresses that there is no link between their riches and their own righteous living or moral uprightness. He then proceeds to his most valuable insight by pointing out that wealth is one of the key 'sacraments' of the *old* covenant between God and his people, thus being a sign of the relationship into which he has called them by his grace.

He explains the use of this sacrament for those who live under the old covenant: 'We are . . . called to use our wealth so that our actions announce to the watching world that election is free, that grace is abundant, that a new creation is promised and that God owns all things.'[3] These four truths would, I imagine, be at the heart of the firm convictions held by those many Christians today who claim unalloyed health, wealth and success for the children of God.

But Ellul will not allow us to rest there.

> Jesus Christ strips wealth of the sacramental character that we have recognized in the Old Testament . . . wealth no longer expresses spiritual truth because the fullness of grace resides in Christ. What would the gift of wealth mean now that God has given us his Son? He is now our only wealth . . . Wealth is no longer a sacrament because 'God chose what is weak in the world to shame the strong' (1 Cor 1:27). In Christ God chooses what has no intrinsic value and makes it adequate to the work he is undertaking. This work must not be done by human hands. It must not be possible for anyone to thank a particular method for what is solely an action of grace. Wealth by itself is an economic power, and because it is a power, it is now rejected . . . Wealth, then, is reduced to money. And money has no place in the work of redemption.[4]

The power of Mammon

We can better appreciate now, I believe, why 'the Incarnation of Jesus Christ totally modifies our perspective'.[5] We can also understand why the teaching of Jesus (as, indeed, that of the whole New Testament) is almost without exception entirely negative about money and wealth. It also becomes apparent why in two powerful contexts we read of material possessions being personified as 'Mammon' – i.e. recognised as having personal power, able to control our lives, and to become a rival master for our allegiance over against God himself. Money, possessions, wealth are all outward, physical manifestations of this spiritual power, Mammon, 'a power which tries to be like God'[6] in competing for our loyalty.

Unless we appreciate that money and possessions are the raw material by which Mammon actively tempts us away from obedience to God, we multiply our vulnerability to Satan in his determination to pollute the power which Christians have received as sons and daughters of God. The personification of Mammon by Jesus indicates that it is one of the 'principalities and powers' – originally created for the glory of God, then involved in Satan's arrogant snatching at equality with God, now exposed and defeated through the death and resurrection of Jesus – which will ultimately be forced to relinquish their hold on God's people and God's possessions, before being finally destroyed by Jesus before he 'delivers the kingdom to God the Father' (1 Cor 15:24). By its incessant use of money, Mammon works, as did Satan himself with Jesus, for our worship.

In this perspective, the words of Jesus in the sermon on the mount assume even more devastating meaning. He declared: 'No one can serve two masters; for either he will hate the one and love the other, or he will be devoted to the one and despise the other. You cannot serve God and mammon' (Matt 6:24). Any surrender to Mammon signifies the true devotion of our hearts – 'Either God is served with a single-eyed devotion, or he is not served at all. Attempts at divided loyalty betray, not partial commitment to discipleship, but deep-seated commitment to idolatry.'[7]

This is the moment to return to Paul's oft-quoted (and misquoted) words: 'For the love of money is the root of all evils' (1 Tim 6:10). In terms of Jesus' words on two masters, the truth is painfully apparent: love of money equals hatred of God. When Paul therefore calls love of money the root of all evils, it is 'not a hackneyed bit of popular morality': it 'is an accurate summary of this conflict'[8] between God and

Mammon. The problem of materialism has, therefore, to be tackled at its root – in our hearts, where we let either God or Mammon possess us.

Going to the heart

Jesus' attitude to money consistently goes to the heart. A few examples will make this clear. When a man from the crowds asked Jesus to sort out problems over a legacy, Jesus first refused to act as arbitrator and then taught everyone within reach about the perils of covetousness (Luke 12:13–21). No doubt he could have adjudicated with fairness and accuracy in this dispute between two brothers about their father's inheritance – apparently rabbis were often consulted about such matters. But Jesus was far more concerned to get to the heart of the matter. It is quite possible that the man's complaint against his brother was legitimate, that he was being defrauded of his rights. By his attitude to such a situation Jesus reinforces his teaching elsewhere that God looks on the heart, that it ultimately matters little whether we get our rights over material things or not, unless we have been released from the grip of greed, the mastery of Mammon.

More than that, according to the parable about the rich fool which expands Jesus' warning against all forms of covetousness, we are completely senseless if we pour our energies into worldly affairs and neglect our relationship with God – 'God said to him, "Fool!" . . . So is he who lays up treasure for himself, and is not rich toward God' (Luke 12:20–21). The key phrases in this sentence are 'for himself' and 'toward God'. How much time and effort do we spend nurturing our relationship with the Lord, compared with what we expend in making life more pleasant and comfortable for ourselves? We fool ourselves – probably the essence of foolishness – when we fail to recognise the immense power of material possessions to erode and to expel trust in God.

Because Jesus detected greed in the heart of the man who talked to him about his inheritance, he was going to do nothing even to establish that greed more firmly within him, let alone increase it. He refused to arbitrate in such a dispute because he was concerned for the man's true 'life', which 'does not consist in the abundance of his possessions' (Luke 12:15). Until we, like Jesus, see such greed as straightforward idolatry (Col 3:5) (i.e. worship of Mammon in the place of God, and therefore transgression of the first commandment), we are likely both to rationalise our own love of money and encourage the same radical opposition to God in others. 'What will it profit a man, if he gains the whole world and forfeits his life?' (Matt 16:26). It is a fact of mere observation that wealth eats away at faith in God more thoroughly and pervasively than poverty.

Covetousness or greed are not, of course, the prerogative of the wealthy. Every person, rich and poor, knows in their heart the pull to possess more and more. The spiritual power of Mammon reveals itself in the fact that the more we have the more we want. There is nothing truly satisfying in the possession of material things. Mammon, in other words, promises life with a capital 'L', but it actually never produces it, because it cannot do so.

A second incident from Luke's gospel illustrates the truths of this first story, the description of the rich man and Lazarus (Luke 16:19–31). Using imagery familiar to his contemporary audience, Jesus issues a dire warning to those who, like the Pharisees (to whom Luke has referred a moment earlier), are 'lovers of money' (Luke 16:14). The climax of the story is the complete reversal of fortunes – the rich man enduring the torments of Hades, the poor man enjoying the eternal security of 'Abraham's bosom'. The rich man had stored up treasure for himself, and this habitual approach to his possessions turned him into a hard, insensitive, unsympathetic person. He became like the things he loved – money and possessions. That is the power of money, and Jesus wanted people to be under no illusions about it. In terms of what he could personally enjoy, the rich man had gained the whole world: but he had forfeited real life, forfeited eternal life in this world and the next, because he was devoted to Mammon (the other appearance of the saying 'You cannot serve God and mammon' occurs a few verses earlier, Luke 16:13). By this devotion he transgressed the two great commandments – to love God with his whole heart and soul and mind and strength, and to love his neighbour (Lazarus) as he loved himself.

The rich man's love of money made him hard towards Lazarus, but also blind towards God and his own spiritual condition. He becomes, in the teaching of Jesus as set out in Luke's gospel, a pointer to the blindness of the Pharisees, the archetypal 'lovers of money' at the time of Jesus. This blindness to their own spiritual condition is one of the many haunting refrains in Jesus' woes on the Pharisees: 'Woe to you, blind guides' (Matt 23:16, 17, 24, 26). We will be looking more thoroughly at Jesus' contacts with the Pharisees in the next chapter. At this stage we need only note how he describes each of them as a 'child of hell' (Matt 23:15), an eloquent echo of the rich man's torments in Hades. Equally, he calls them 'blind fools' (Matt 23:17), clearly reminiscent of God's words to the rich man in the earlier story, 'You fool!' The power of Mammon makes us fatally foolish about what really matters: it deprives us of our reason.

This inexorable exposé of the power of money continues in the story of the rich young ruler (Luke 18:18–30; cf. Matt 19:16–30; Mark 10:17–31). The general impression given of this man by all three synoptic gospels is not of a demonstrably covetous or callous person – not, at any rate, like the two men in our previous two incidents. The problem went deeper – to his heart. He had great possessions, genuinely lived a decent life – including trying to love his neighbours as himself. But the man could not give up his possessions when Jesus told him to do so. He had asked Jesus what he had to do in order to 'inherit eternal life', Jesus told him to sell his possessions and give to the poor, then 'come, follow me' (Luke 18:22). Yet he could not do it. Mammon had him by the throat, in his heart, across the board. He was devoted to Mammon – respectably, attractively, religiously . . . but fatally.

The need to be set free

It is when Jesus touches our material possessions and tells us to relinquish them that the power of money becomes apparent. Jacques Ellul writes of the rich young ruler:

He can of course use it [his money] morally; that solves nothing. He remains bound to this power, and Jesus shows him his real situation . . . What is condemned here is the power of money and not the man . . . [Jesus' command is given] to show that he is weak, a slave; that money is a power; that man's strength is unable to free him; that he needs Jesus' intervention and grace.[9]

This is God's judgment on the man, a judgment *for* him, not against him: he wants to save him and make him live. This is the importance and the value of those words 'come, follow me'. Only by following Jesus, along with his other disciples, would the man find 'the expulsive power of a new affection' replacing the tyranny of Mammon with the love of God as expressed in the fellowship of those who were following Jesus. Mark points us to this key truth in his moving comment: 'Jesus looking upon him loved him' (Mark 10:21).

The vital lessons in this encounter are underlined, in counterpoint, by the story of Zacchaeus (Luke 19:1–10). Incidentally, the fact that Zacchaeus did not give away *all* his possessions and yet according to Jesus is the recipient of salvation ought to scotch any universalisation of the command to the rich young ruler to 'Sell all that you have' (Luke 18:22). Here was another wealthy man – probably neither young nor a ruler – who *was* able to respond to the call of Jesus, who chose to give half of his goods to the poor and to repay fourfold those whom he had defrauded, who was released from his bondage to Mammon by the love of Jesus in inviting himself to the home of 'a sinner'.

The conversion of Zacchaeus from being one of Mammon's prize exhibits in Jericho to being a joyful disciple of Jesus is Luke's way of answering the disciples' confusion, anxiety and suppressed anger at Jesus' attitude to the rich young ruler. As Jesus watched the young man walk sadly away, he said: 'How hard it is for those who have riches to enter the kingdom of God! For it is easier for a camel to go through the eye of a needle than for a rich man to enter the kingdom of God' (Luke 18:24–25). The disciples knew how hard it was for anyone with worldly possessions simply to get rid of them: they exclaimed, 'Then who can be saved?' (Luke 18:26).

Zacchaeus was God's answer, proving that 'What is impossible with men is possible with God' (Luke 18:27). The love of
Jesus was able to break through the bondage of Mammon and
set the little tax collector free: he received Jesus 'joyfully'
(Luke 19:6). The disciples had despairingly said, 'Then who
can be saved?'; Jesus waited a day or two, then took the
initiative of love 'to seek and to save' the most unlikely and
impossible person in Jericho, and then declared: 'Today
salvation has come to this house' (Luke 19:9). If salvation can
come to *this* house and *this* person, then *all* things are
possible: Jesus is able 'for all time to save those who draw near
to God through him' (Heb 7:25).

The rich fool in the parable, the rich man who ignored
Lazarus, the rich young ruler who turned away from Jesus,
the rich tax collector in Jericho, the Pharisees who were
lovers of money – all were 'lost'. Jesus came to seek and to
save such lost people. To do that, he had to destroy the works
of the devil: that includes breaking the bondage of Mammon,
as part and parcel of Jesus' continuing conflict with Satan. The
betrayal of Jesus by Judas Iscariot marks the final act in this
conflict.

> It is not insignificant that Judas's act is represented as a
> purchased act . . . Judas's betrayal would not be complete
> if it were not the fruit of the conflict between Satan and
> Jesus . . . Satan had to bring all his powers into play: the
> power of violence with the soldiers, the power of the law
> with the high priest, the power of money with the thirty
> pieces of silver.[10]

Judas was by this stage in the grip of Satan. Luke's narrative
is explicit about this:

> Then Satan entered into Judas called Iscariot, who was of
> the number of the twelve; he went away and conferred
> with the chief priests and officers how he might betray
> [Jesus] to them. And they were glad, and engaged to give
> him money. So he agreed, and sought an opportunity
> to betray him to them in the absence of the multitude
> (Luke 22:3–6).

Satan used one of his most powerful minions, Mammon, to clinch Judas' treachery. It is likely that Judas had also hoped that Jesus would be a powerful political Messiah. Satan capitalised on that desire, which had been his major tactic at the outset in the wilderness. He then used Judas' love of money to propel him along the path of his (i.e. Satan's) ultimate purpose – the destruction of Jesus. Matthew's account clearly demonstrates this, because he explains that Judas went to the chief priests and said, 'What will you give me if I deliver him to you?' (Matt 26:15). The money was not incidental, it was the ultimately powerful incentive.

John, describing events at Bethany in the home of Mary, Martha and Lazarus only a few days before the betrayal, makes it plain that Judas had been powerless to resist the demands of Mammon for a long time. When 'Mary took a pound of costly ointment of pure nard and anointed the feet of Jesus and wiped his feet with her hair' (John 12:3), Judas complained about the extreme wastefulness of such an ex- travagant act of devotion. The ointment was worth the annual wages of a labourer and if sold the proceeds could have been given to the poor, he said. John comments: 'This he said, not that he cared for the poor but because he was a thief, and as he had the money box he used to take what was put into it' (John 12:6). Judas, acting according to the dictates of the one who ruled his life, was a greedy, snatching, grasping man – even taking for himself what was intended to be given away to those in need. Jesus became the victim of this greed.

The story of Judas therefore shows the power of money in three ways: the power which the chief priests exercised over Judas because they possessed money and were prepared to use it for their own ends; the power which the love of money exercised over Judas; and the power which money exercised in the arrest and crucifixion of Jesus. It is this last perspective which must now begin to command our attention, because it is Jesus' very submission to this 'purchased act' of betrayal which points the way to a truly Christian attitude to money. As Ellul says, 'because the Son of God was thus turned into merchandise, all subordination of humankind to money is intolerable'.[11]

The deepest reason why this is intolerable lies in the true

significance of Jesus' death. Peter captured it well in these
words: 'You . . . were ransomed . . . not with perishable
things such as silver or gold, but with the precious blood of
Christ' (1 Pet 1:18–19). We have been redeemed from bondage to Satan and Mammon at an infinite cost – the blood of
God's only Son. This freedom to serve God in Christ is the
ultimate gift of God's grace. We have been transferred from a
kingdom where greed, grasping, snatching and robbery prevail, into a kingdom where grace, giving, serving and sharing
prevail. It cost us nothing to be transferred from one kind of
power to the other. It cost Jesus not merely his life but
'subordination to money', being turned into a piece of merchandise. 'Satan can claim to have put God under his own
law, the law of selling', but 'God pays the price so that he can
give freedom and act in *grace*'.[12]

In and through Jesus we have entered a totally new world,
where 'nothing is for sale; everything is given away. The mark
of the world of money . . . is the exact opposite of the mark of
God's world where everything is free, where giving is the
normal way to act . . . Mammon's work is the exact opposite
of God's work'.[13] By the paradoxical combination of a refusal
to submit to Satan's attempts to *lure* him into a selfish and
snatching attitude to power, and a willing submission to
Satan's successful use of those methods through those involved in his arrest, trial and crucifixion, Jesus has purchased
(actually, bought *back*) the world and everything in it for free
enjoyment by his redeemed people. How are we to use the
money and other material possessions thus regained by Jesus?
By his teaching and example Jesus seems to give us at least
four principles.

Be quietly relaxed

First, we show our freedom from the tyranny of Mammon by
being quietly relaxed about material possessions and the
money that can purchase them for us. The teaching of Jesus
on this is unenigmatic and familiar: 'I tell you, do not be
anxious about your life, what you shall eat, nor about your
body, what you shall put on' (Luke 12:22). He urges us to look

around us: the birds of the air are fed through the care of God – and they do not work long hours or put up large houses. Consider the flowers growing up all around us without any effort or labour: who but God gives them their beauty and attractiveness? If God spends such time and attention on birds and flowers, 'how much more will he clothe you, O men of little faith! And do not seek what you are to eat and what you are to drink, nor be of anxious mind. For all the nations of the world seek these things; and your Father knows that you need them' (Luke 12:28–30).

This account of Jesus' teaching on this subject is taken from Luke's gospel and follows immediately after the parable of the rich fool. The opposite of being covetous and foolishly unprepared for eternity is to be quietly released in the loving care of our heavenly Father, who can be completely trusted to provide what we need. Anxiety arises as a result of having our minds set on things, worrying about what God has undertaken to provide for us. We are to set our minds on 'the kingdom of God', to be concerned with the way God's power is exercised – i.e. by giving, serving, sharing. By such single-minded attention to the dynamics of God's kingdom, we will be automatically turning our backs on the snatching, greedy elements of the world where Mammon rules. The word translated 'anxious' has the literal connotation of being divided up into little pieces. As we have noticed before, the impact of Satan's activity is always to scatter, divide, disperse. Jesus wants to integrate our lives and centre them on the kingdom of God.

The perverse aspect of this anxiety, which Jesus orders us to lay aside, is that it seems to take possession of poor and not so poor alike. The questions 'What shall we eat? What shall we drink? What shall we wear?' (Matt 6:31) are on the lips of all sorts and conditions of men and women. For the truly poor, the anxiety is to find the *next* meal or a pair of shoes. For the more affluent, the anxiety manifests itself over *which* options of many to choose for the next meal or day. Again we can see the grip which Mammon holds on us: mere possession does not diminish anxiety. Indeed, as Jesus points out, it may actually increase it, because 'moth and rust consume and . . . thieves break in and steal' (Matt 6:19).

For Jesus, the ability to be quietly relaxed about material necessities derived from his trust in his Father. He knew God to be as he taught his disciples to believe him to be – a heavenly Father who knows that we need all these things. He was not, therefore, driven by worry about meals, drink or clothes. When he was genuinely hungry he knew how to feed on the promises of God not to let him starve to death (Matt 4:4). When his disciples urged him to take time to eat a proper meal he told them – somewhat cryptically – that 'I have food to eat of which you do not know' (John 4:32). When they wondered who had surreptitiously slipped him a sandwich, he went on: 'My food is to do the will of him who sent me, and to accomplish his work' (John 4:34). At the same time, he was sufficiently relaxed to accept the generosity of some wealthy women who looked after his needs, as well as the hospitality provided by Mary, Martha and Lazarus in their Bethany home (cf. Luke 8:3; John 12:1–2).

If money was needed for any particular occasion, he trusted his Father in heaven to provide whatever was necessary – perhaps this is the underlying point of the strange incident about paying the half-shekel tax by finding it in the mouth of a fish (Matt 17:24–27). Jesus wanted, in any case, to stress that 'the sons [of the kingdom of God] are free' – and the story certainly reinforces the relaxed freedom from such cares which Jesus clearly knew.

As Jesus intimated to his disciples, every one of his followers can have the same quiet assurance about the Father's provision for our needs, if we singlemindedly concern ourselves with the work he has given us to do – the work of the kingdom of God. In referring to himself as 'the bread of life', Jesus was teaching the same lesson: 'he who comes to me shall not hunger, and he who believes in me shall never thirst . . . I am the living bread which came down from heaven; if any one eats of this bread, he will live for ever; and the bread which I shall give for the life of the world is my flesh' (John 6:35, 51). In giving us himself, Jesus has given us bread which will sustain us in eternal life – and that promise and provision includes what we need to sustain physical life, for as long as God has his work for us to do on this earth. As George Whitefield once put it, we are immortal until our work is done; death cannot touch us until God's purpose for our earthly life has been accomplished.

Be lavishly generous

If the first principle with regard to a Christian use of money is to be quietly relaxed about our needs, the second is to be lavishly generous in our giving. Ellul is at his most pungent on this subject. He urges us to make money profane by uprooting its sacred character and thereby destroying the element of power in money: 'There is one act par excellence which profanes money by going directly against the law of money . . . This act is *giving*.'[14] He points out that, according to Paul, money is made by Christians *in order* to be given away – 'God is able to provide you with every blessing in abundance, so that you may always have enough of everything and may provide in abundance for every good work' (2 Cor 9:8).

When, therefore, we have enough, the rest is for us to give away with lavish generosity. As to what is enough, there will clearly be divergent estimates, and Jesus seems to lay down no law, except that we should be joyfully ready to give what we have to those who do not (Matt 5:42). At times this giving will be difficult for others to understand, indeed easy for them to misinterpret. This is most apparent in the action of Mary in pouring perfume over Jesus at the Bethany home whose hospitality he appreciated so much (Matt 26:6–13). When the disciples, including Judas, complained about the wastefulness of this lavish action, Jesus warmly praised Mary for her generosity and love. If giving away our money and the things we possess profanes what the world has made sacred, such giving to God is the supreme act of profanation. 'Giving to God introduces the useless into the world of efficiency',[15] says Ellul, 'We need to regain an appreciation of gifts that are not utilitarian.'[16]

There will also be the very rare occasion when such lavish generosity will appear completely senseless, if not foolishly dangerous. We certainly cannot give what we do not have (although modern methods of credit and accountancy can encourage both individuals and local churches to take this

slippery path); but God may be looking for us to give everything we do have – just this once, or on this particular
occasion.

This seems to be the force of the incident at the temple in
Jerusalem, when Jesus

> sat down opposite the treasury, and watched the multitude
> putting money into the treasury. Many rich people put in
> large sums. And a poor widow came, and put in two copper
> coins, which make a penny. And he called his disciples to
> him, and said to them, 'Truly, I say to you, this poor widow
> has put in more than all those who are contributing to the
> treasury. For they all contributed out of their abundance;
> but she out of her poverty has put in everything she had, her
> whole living.' (Mark 12:41–44)

Ellul thinks that Jesus deliberately sat down to watch
people giving to the temple treasury – 'This implies then that
we must pass under Jesus' scrutiny each time we handle
money.'[17] It would certainly appear that the woman's lavish
generosity, which was presumably not known by anyone else
except Jesus, was deliberately described and explained to the
disciples in order to press home the way that giving sometimes
will bear no relation to the dictates of pragmatic common
sense. The widow could not afford to give everything away,
but she did. Only Jesus was aware of it, and he rejoiced: here
was a woman who understood that grace is at the heart of the
kingdom of God, that 'It is more blessed to give than to
receive' (Acts 20:35).

The wonderful example of lavish generosity provided by
the widow at the temple treasury took place very soon after
Jesus' driving of the moneychangers out of the temple (Mark
11:15–19). If, as seems likely, the two incidents happened
fairly close together, we can appreciate the way the one action
rejoiced the Lord's heart, while the desecration of the temple
by profiteers angered him. The woman was providing a model
of what it means to give because we have received grace upon
grace; the moneychangers were using every opportunity to
make a fat profit for themselves by snatching all they could
out of the hands of the worshippers. Both actions took place

in the temple precincts, 'my Father's house' (Luke 2:49), in the place set apart for 'the God of all grace' (1 Pet 5:10). Jesus was peremptory with the moneychangers, not only because they had turned God's house into 'a den of robbers' who were making a profit out of the poor, but because they were using God's house as the shrine of Mammon.

Jesus refers to the word of the Lord through the prophet Isaiah: 'My house shall be called a house of prayer for all the nations' (Mark 11:17). That statement of intent comes in the middle of a passage which anticipates the Lord's gathering together not only of 'the outcasts of Israel' but of 'foreigners' to 'my holy mountain', where he will 'make them joyful in my house of prayer' (Isa 56:7–8). This glorious future is, in its turn, preceded by one of the classic invitations from the Lord: 'Ho, every one who thirsts, come to the waters; and he who has no money, come, buy and eat! Come, buy wine and milk without money and without price' (Isa 55:1). This open invitation, full of God's grace and generosity, will result in God's people being renewed: 'Behold, you shall call nations that you know not, and nations that knew you not shall run to you, because of the Lord your God' (Isa 55:5). Then the temple would become 'a house of prayer for all the nations'.

This was the future which the moneychangers in the temple were desecrating; this was the future which the widow at the treasury was foreshadowing. In Jesus the invitation to the thirsty and the moneyless had been issued. Salvation is free and sets people free – free to give and free to serve. Only those gripped by their own privileges, rights and merits could begrudge the Lord his lavish generosity (cf. Matt 20:1–16, esp. 15). Those humble enough to receive his grace would be unlocked to give, and go on giving – even when it seems senseless: 'Freely you have received, freely give' (Matt 10:8 NIV).

Be shrewdly wise

The third principle in using money Christianly is contained in the context surrounding the parable of the unjust steward (Luke 16:1–15). It is the need to be shrewdly wise in the

strategic deployment of our material resources. Luke locates
Jesus' words about the two rival masters, God and Mammon,
in this context. One of the ways, therefore, in which we can
establish the sovereign rule of Jesus over all rebellious principalities and powers is by making 'friends for [ourselves] by
means of unrighteous mammon, so that when it fails they may
receive [us] into the eternal habitations' (Luke 16:9).

The money we have, as Christians, is to be invested wisely
in people whom God can use and is using in his kingdom. This
will include evangelistic ministry, missionary outreach
throughout the world, training and teaching of Christian
disciples and those destined to exercise responsibility in
God's church, compassionate work among the poor and
deprived, and a multitude of other ministries along the guidelines set by Jesus himself in his ministry. We will be equally
concerned about *both* the way the money is used *and* about
the way we make the money available. We will look for
faithful stewardship in others; we will also be determined not
to use our money to bring improper influence to bear on its
recipients. It is always tempting, according to the tenets of
those who serve Mammon, to think that we are entitled to lay
down conditions and dictate to others how they should spend
the money we have given, even how they should lead their
lives.

It is worth stressing that such shrewd use of our material
resources is required by Jesus not just for the money we set
apart explicitly for such kingdom purposes but for everything
we own. If it does not cover everything, we are allowing
Mammon to retain its hold on us. But we cannot serve two
masters. Jesus stresses this in the teaching which follows the
parable of the unjust steward, when he mentions the need to
be 'faithful in a very little' (Luke 16:10). If we move out of
such faithfulness in even a tiny fraction of our lives, we allow
what Jesus calls unrighteousness – i.e. the characteristics of
Mammon – to infiltrate the whole (or 'much').

Be personally vulnerable

Be quietly relaxed, be lavishly generous, be shrewdly wise –
and be personally vulnerable: this principle is proclaimed not

so much by the direct teaching of Jesus as by his whole living and dying. He gave healing, deliverance, teaching, encouragement, wisdom, forgiveness, joy, but supremely he gave himself. This was the truth which the Christians in Macedonia, in extreme poverty, had learnt (2 Cor 8:1–5): 'first they gave themselves . . . to us by the will of God' then they gave money 'beyond their means, of their own free will'. The Macedonian Christians made themselves – as well as their money – available to Paul and his colleagues.

Even Paul admitted that the totally vulnerable self-giving of these poor Christians had taken him by surprise. It is a rare and precious experience to be on the receiving end of such unconditional, unpressurising and sacrificial generosity. They had taken their inspiration from Jesus himself, who, 'though he was rich, yet for your sake he became poor, so that by his poverty you might become rich' (2 Cor 8:9). That was 'the grace of our Lord Jesus Christ', and grace does not use gifts as a protective screen behind which we hide our real selves.

Whenever money is separated either from the people who earn and make it or from the people who receive and give it, the influence of the god Mammon can be detected. At the level of industrial relations, the employer 'must come to the point of considering workers as neighbors'.[18] In other personal relationships, this principle urges us not to allow material possessions to shut people off from one another, to divide people, to 'scatter'. Our giving is to reflect the giving of ourselves in loving service, not manipulating or snatching in the style of Mammon but giving according to the pattern of Jesus.

7 THE GUARDIANS OF TRADITION – RELIGIOUS POWER

Palestine at the time of Jesus was a country riddled with religion, but its people were 'harassed and helpless, like sheep without a shepherd' (Matt 9:36). Jesus was clearly anguished by this situation and, according to the four evangelists, unashamedly tackled head-on those whom he regarded as responsible for this spiritual desolation. His most uncompromising criticisms were levelled at the religious hierarchy, both official and unofficial, of the day. Let us take a look at these men.

At the top of the ladder was the high priest, the most important single individual in the nation. Under Jewish law this man was authorised to make atonement for the sins of the whole people. He also presided over the Sanhedrin, a council of seventy (perhaps seventy-two) leading men in Jerusalem. Although the arrival of the Romans in 63 BC and the succession of Herods as king seriously undermined the overall authority of the Sanhedrin, and of the high priest in particular, this religious hierarchy still held immense power in the land. The high priest represented the Jewish people in any dealings with Rome and his own personal influence was virtually unassailable.

Under the high priest there were eleven chief priests, an élite who had great riches and great power in a city which was based on its religious importance. They were responsible for the temple, including both the direction of the daily services and the administration of its massive finances. When Jesus whipped the moneychangers and merchants out of the temple precincts, he was directly challenging the authority of the chief priests.

The rest of the Sanhedrin was comprised of scribes (who were experts in the law of Moses) and elders (who were men of great wealth from the most influential families in the land). The mood of the Sanhedrin at any one period of time depended on the strength of the particular 'parties' in the council: in the years immediately preceding the public ministry of Jesus there had been a gradual erosion of the power of the Sadducees in favour of the Pharisees. The Sadducees were essentially an upper-class minority who attempted to preserve the purity of Judaism in the distinctiveness of its priestly caste – if the priests in general were of the right calibre and commitment, the integrity of the nation was reckoned to be secure. They kept strictly to the written code of the Old Testament scriptures.

The traditions of the elders

The Pharisees, on the other hand, saw external purity of life as necessary for ordinary people, not just the priests. They developed a wide range of additional regulations ('the traditions of the elders') alongside the written law of Moses. They called for rigid adherence to these by everyone: in this important sense, they were a populist movement standing over against the wealthy, priestly trends of the Sadducees. By the time of Jesus they had virtually commandeered the positions of religious power in the country. Most of the scribes were probably Pharisees, and such men were highly educated: we read of such individuals questioning and challenging Jesus over exegetical matters to do with the law (cf. Matt 15:1–9; Mark 2:16; 7:1–13; 12:28; Luke 5:30). Nicodemus was probably a scribe belonging to the party of the Pharisees, as were Gamaliel and Saul of Tarsus. Likewise, many of the priests would also have belonged to the party of the Pharisees. In general, however, we need to remember that the ordinary Pharisee was a straightforward layman, with the scribes being the equivalent of theologians – whichever 'party' they espoused.

In the gospel narratives we sometimes read of 'the scribes', sometimes of 'the Pharisees', occasionally of 'the scribes of the Pharisees', frequently of 'the scribes and the Pharisees'. If we bear in mind the distinctions explained above, we can see that the different language describes a variety of religious affiliation or emphasis, but an awesome concentration of religious power – official and unofficial – in an extremely influential minority. The scribes were the theological experts who, by dint of total application to studying the law, had made themselves men of immense power. They alone were reckoned to have knowledge of the deepest secrets of the divine being, passing them on only in secret to their pupils. As Pharisaical tenets came into theological fashion among the scribes, so these pupils became unofficial models of piety – held in awe and admiration (tinged with not a little resentment) by ordinary Jews.

One of the paradoxical – though understandable – realities of Pharisaism was the immense following secured among the ordinary men and women of the country. Every town and village had its quota of Pharisees. By their beliefs and practices they isolated themselves from ordinary people and there was a vast chasm between the two. Yet their power was immense, not least because the Pharisaic position was overtly linked with a strident nationalism which stressed Jewish purity in the midst of Roman occupation. 'The Pharisees were the real religious leaders of the nation.'[1]

The charges levelled by Jesus

Against this backcloth we can more readily appreciate the thrust of Jesus' encounters with the scribes and the Pharisees, in particular the verbal onslaught he often unleashed against them. Jesus treated them as the ones holding religious power, whether official and ordained or unofficial and theologically uneducated: 'The scribes and the Pharisees sit on Moses' seat' (Matt 23:2). Whether they had actually chased this power (as many had from a very young age) or had gradually found themselves assuming it, Jesus consistently confronted them with its responsibilities. Matthew 23 highlights this confrontation in a sequence of pungent charges. The dangers inherent in holding religious power are exposed in this chapter: there is little reason to suppose that these dangers have changed, let alone disappeared in the last two thousand years.

Imposing heavy burdens

The first accusation Jesus brings is that 'they preach, but do not practise' (Matt 23:3). In so doing, 'They bind heavy burdens, hard to bear, and lay them on men's shoulders' (Matt 23:4). The list of such obligations was endless, covering every last detail of daily life. This 'tradition of the elders', orally transmitted from scribe to pupil and binding on everyone, turned living into a miserable steeplechase, in which ordinary people were constantly trying to keep this or that regulation – or be duly punished. They were carrying extremely heavy burdens, from which there was never any promise of release. Certainly the Pharisees themselves never lifted a finger to help such burdened souls. The net result was a society riddled with religious guilt for having broken rules and regulations manufactured by the scribes and Pharisees. To such weary and heavy-laden souls Jesus offered rest and refreshment: 'Come to me, all who labour and are heavy laden, and I will give you rest' (Matt 11:28).

Nobody could possibly have perfectly kept 'the tradition of the elders', neither the Pharisees nor even their scribes. The regulations governing the sabbath provide a good example. The law (or Torah) said a man must not do any work on the sabbath; the traditions (the Halakah) laid down how many paces a man might walk, how heavy a burden he might carry. In fact thirty-nine basic actions which constituted work were laid down as forbidden on the sabbath. For example, it was forbidden to go on a journey, to till a farm, to light a fire, to ride a beast, to strike, catch or kill an animal or a bird, to fast or to make war.

In such ways the great principles of the law were broken up into thousands of petty rules and regulations. 'By the time [these] scribal interpretation[s] of the Law [were] finished, it took more than fifty volumes to hold the mass of regulations which resulted.'[2] This was the burden the Pharisee earnestly undertook to carry – and zealously sought to impose on others. He had managed to turn religion into an intolerable burden. William Barclay has posed some searching questions for modern examples of Pharisaism: 'Does it make [religion] a joy or a depression? Is a man helped by his religion or is he haunted by it? Does it carry him, or has he to carry it?'[3]

Because the Pharisees and their scribes would not allow the slightest relaxation, let alone removal, of these man-made regulations, the burden on ordinary people became heavier and heavier. When those who possess religious power over the many turn countless lives into such misery, the explosive anger of Jesus remains equally virulent.

The need to impress

The second charge Jesus brings against the scribes and the Pharisees is similarly direct: 'They do all their deeds to be seen by men' (Matt 23:5). They took an inordinate pride in outward symbols of their piety, in their phylacteries and their fringes (or tassels). Normally the phylacteries were small boxes that were worn on the arm or attached to the forehead and which contained a piece of vellum inscribed with four texts from the law. It is likely that by the time of Jesus these were used in a semi-magical sense, like charms or amulets. The scribes and the Pharisees made theirs as large as possible, simply in order to impress people with their piety. The same went for the tassels worn by every Jew, including Jesus (cf. Matt 9:20; 14:36), which the scribes and Pharisees made as long as possible.

Their determination to impress everyone spilt over into virtually every part of life: when they went into the synagogues, they insisted on having 'the best seats'; when they attended banquets and other special celebrations, they expected 'the place of honour' (Matt 23:6). Walking around the streets, they required special greetings from ordinary folk to befit their prestige and power. Jesus pinpointed the basic problem: they loved all these things – their hearts were set upon them and they were the things which really mattered. Status, recognition, special treatment – the best of everything – these were the priorities of the scribes and Pharisees.

According to the sermon on the mount, they were so enslaved by this need to impress everyone that it affected ordinary religious actions like praying, fasting and alms-giving. In each case, affirmed Jesus, they acted in order to 'be seen by men' (Matt 6:2, 5, 16). They had lost any proper or genuine God-consciousness, even in praying. This is presumably the significance of Jesus' masterly throwaway line in telling the parable of the Pharisee and the tax collector: 'The Pharisee stood and prayed thus with himself . . .' (Luke 18:11).

The exclusivist mentality
The third charge Jesus brought was that they were 'blind guides' (Matt 23:16). They had set themselves up as the experts on virtually everything to do with Jewish life and belief, but in fact they had concocted a living hell for their followers and for themselves (Matt 23:15). They had, by their legalistic nitpicking, turned the kingdom of heaven into an impregnable fortress. They had made the terms of entry so strict that no one could get in. Whereas they fondly imagined that they, and they alone, held 'the key of knowledge' (cf. Luke 11:52) to let people into the kingdom of God, in fact they had long since forfeited any right to enter it themselves. They had become culpably blind leaders of the innocently blind multitudes. The fact they were so keen on making proselytes for their sectarian, exclusivist, separatist dogmas (Matt 23:15) served merely to heighten the seriousness of their abuse of the religious power they had assumed.

This blindness had entirely warped their judgment: they regarded the gold in the temple as more sacred than the temple itself (Matt 23:16–17), the gift on the altar as more binding in oathtaking than the altar itself (Matt 23:18–19). This speciousness had the practical effect of encouraging sheer flippancy in making promises and in speaking the truth. What had no doubt started as an attempt by the scribes and Pharisees to repress thoughtless oathtaking by ordinary people with less than a proper awe for holy things and holy places, had degenerated into a licence for lying and dishonesty – all in the name of religion.

Just as the prayers of the Pharisees had become horizontal soliloquies, marked by much talk about God but no relationship with God, so their pontifications about oaths, vows and promises had effectively removed from everyday conversation any proper consciousness among ordinary people of the God of truth (Matt 23:20–22). With the sanction of their religious leaders men and women evaded the responsibility to speak and live the truth with one another . . . and gave a pious rationalisation for such dishonesty.

Trivial pursuits
Fourthly, Jesus charges the scribes and Pharisees with neglecting 'the weightier matters of the law' (Matt 23:23). They had been so caught up with sheer trivial pursuits – for example, being meticulous about laying aside a tenth of their spice-rack – that they had completely abandoned the heart of the law: justice, mercy and faithfulness. Jesus acknowledges that if the law required careful tithing (and there was actually no plain injunction to tithe your spices and herbs), then that command should not have been neglected: but 'to act justly and to love mercy and to walk humbly with your God' (Mic 6:8 NIV) is the Lord's requirement of every person he has made. The Pharisees had become so enmeshed in subsidiary matters that they had allowed the primary commandments to fall by the wayside. They were so intent on observing the minutiae of the law that they had missed the massive priorities which undergirded the whole system. In the memorable words of Jesus, they were 'straining out a gnat and swallowing a camel' (Matt 23:24).

Covering up inner corruption
The fifth charge Jesus levels against these wielders of religious power goes right to the heart of the matter, because it lays bare the essential corruption of every human heart, including the hearts of scribes and Pharisees: 'Woe to you . . . for you are like whitewashed tombs, which outwardly appear beautiful, but within they are full of dead men's bones and all uncleanness. So you also outwardly appear righteous to men, but within you are full of hypocrisy and iniquity' (Matt 23:27–28). In making this assessment, Jesus was not accusing them of being any more corrupt and deceitful than anyone else. This was his verdict on the human heart everywhere in every generation: 'The heart is deceitful above all things, and desperately corrupt' (Jer 17:9).

The scribes and the Pharisees were not prepared to accept

this verdict on humanity. Earlier, Jesus had challenged them about their emphasis on 'the tradition of the elders' over against the word and commandment of God (Matt 15:1–20). They had rebuked Jesus for letting his disciples eat without first washing their hands. Jesus took issue with this insistence on external cleanliness as necessary for purity. The scribes and Pharisees regarded a man to be clean, if he observed the rules and regulations which they laid down. Jesus unequivocally declared that no external ritual can make anyone clean, because we are defiled by what resides inside us – 'out of the heart come evil thoughts, murder, adultery, fornication, theft, false witness, slander. These are what defile a man' (Matt 15:19–20).

Because the power of the scribes and Pharisees virtually depended on ordinary people accepting their rules and regulations about religious and ritual purity, the teaching of Jesus about inner uncleanness posed a dramatic threat to their authority. It is not surprising to read, therefore, that his disciples came to him in a state of some anxiety when they heard him teaching the multitudes that 'not what goes into the mouth defiles a man, but what comes out of the mouth, this defiles a man' (Matt 15:11). Their anxiety was almost tangible – 'Do you know that the Pharisees were offended when they heard this saying?' (Matt 15:12). The disciples could feel the weight of bitter fury on the part of those who wielded such immense religious power. They wanted – one imagines – Jesus to tone his teaching down and not to cause such offence.

Jesus would have nothing of it: he answered uncompromisingly and virtually set up an inevitable confrontation to the death – 'Every plant which my heavenly Father has not planted will be rooted up. Let them alone: they are blind guides. And if a blind man leads a blind man, both will fall into a pit' (Matt 15:13–14). There is absolutely no meeting-point between, on the one hand, men who insist on external rules and regulations as necessary for acceptance before God and, on the other, Jesus – who insists on the essential inner uncleanness of the human heart, with which only he can deal radically enough to create for us a new and living relationship with God as Father.

The scribes and Pharisees did not merely deny the truth

about man's inner corruption, they pretended that they were morally and spiritually pure by virtue of the religious practices they followed – and with which they were constantly impressing others. 'Whitewashed tombs' was the verdict of Jesus on these religious leaders – an assessment only marginally less devastating than his blunt words earlier: 'You brood of vipers! how can you speak good, when you are evil? For out of the abundance of the heart the mouth speaks' (Matt 12:34). Again, we notice that the assumption 'you are evil', made by Jesus of the scribes and Pharisees, is identical with the one he makes in teaching his disciples how to pray: 'If you then, who are evil, know how to give good gifts to your children, how much more will your Father who is in heaven give good things to those who ask him!' (Matt 7:11).

The cancer of hypocrisy

The five charges Jesus brings against the scribes and Pharisees are therefore these: they do not practise what they preach; they run their lives to impress others; they are culpably blind leaders of the people; they neglect what really matters to God; and they cover up their inner rottenness with a copious display of ritual correctness. We can see, then, why Jesus consistently calls them 'hypocrites' – men playing a part, wearing masks to hide their real natures. In fact the religious teachers of Jesus' time were not unaware of the hypocrisy which he so uncompromisingly condemned. There was apparently a current rabbinic saying which went: 'Ninety per cent of all hypocrisy in the world is to be found in Jerusalem.' This hypocrisy Jesus calls 'the leaven in the lump' (Luke 12:1) and tells his own followers, 'Beware . . .' – presumably because of its power to affect everything it touches, and also because of the way it can take a hold on anyone who does not show extreme vigilance. It is easy for any one of the five characteristics of the Pharisees, like leaven or yeast, to infiltrate a disciple of Jesus – all the more so when that disciple is, like the Pharisees, in a position of religious power over others.

It is worth stressing at this point that Jesus warns his

disciples not just of the hypocrisy rampant among the Pharisees but also of the leaven of 'the teaching of the Pharisees and Sadducees' (Matt 16:5–12). A particular trait of the Pharisees was hypocrisy: that kind of *behaviour* is like leaven, according to Jesus. In addition, the actual *teaching* of both the Pharisees and the Sadducees is damaging in its pervasive impact. Both systems had their attraction and their plausibility. Jesus saw the qualities of leaven as much in their teaching as in the behaviour it spawned – a little goes a long way and has devastating effects.

Love of money

Some of the insidious effects of these two kinds of leaven can be traced in the characteristics shown by the scribes and Pharisees, as delineated by the evangelists. For example, in one of the many confrontations between Jesus and the religious leaders Luke comments that the Pharisees were 'lovers of money' (Luke 16:14). Jesus had been stressing to his disciples, and presumably any bystanders within earshot, that 'You cannot serve God and mammon' (Luke 16:13), and that any devotion to the one involves despising the other. The Pharisees were devoted to Mammon, according to Luke, and therefore – in Jesus' diagnosis – despised God. To the Pharisee that whole notion was laughable: of course they were devoted to God, and any faithful Jew could expect God to bless his devotion with lots of Mammon. So, far from God and wealth being rival masters, the one guaranteed the other – in the minds of the Pharisees. Therefore they pursued their religious power as a means of becoming wealthy, imagining that 'religion is a way to become rich' 1 Tim 6:5 GNB) – turning themselves into 'people whose minds do not function and who no longer have the truth'.

Given to conspiracy

The gospels also consistently indicate that the scribes and the Pharisees were inveterate plotters, holding meeting after meeting to work out ways of eliminating Jesus and nullifying the impact of his teaching. After he had trounced them over the issue of sabbath observance 'the Pharisees went out and took counsel against him, how to destroy him' (Matt 12:14). Later they not only took counsel together within their own party, they also consulted with the Herodians (Mark 12:13) and even co-operated with the Sadducees on one occasion (Matt 16:1). Both politically and theologically, the Pharisees were light years away from the Herodians and the Sadducees. But the truth in Jesus turned them into fellow conspirators, who would stop at nothing to prevent their religious power being eroded.

Running scared

The scribes and the Pharisees were also very frightened men, thoroughly scared of the people over whom they exercised such immense power. This became increasingly apparent as they realised that they had to get rid of Jesus if they were to retain their power, but that the people as a whole were likely to be solidly behind Jesus and against them. So we read that 'the chief priests and the elders of the people . . . took counsel . . . to arrest Jesus by stealth and kill him. But they said, "Not during the feast, lest there be a tumult among the people"' (Matt 26:3–5).

Enemies of truth

We have already noticed, in addition, that the scribes and the Pharisees were not concerned for the truth. This became blatant when the hierarchy strove to establish charges against Jesus. The events which passed for a trial demonstrated their opposition to truth. 'The chief priests and the whole council sought false testimony against Jesus that they might put him to death' (Matt 26:59). When Judas Iscariot brought back the thirty pieces of silver (his payment from the chief priests for securing the arrest of Jesus), they ignored the implicit charge against them of wanting to shed 'innocent blood' and were more concerned with ceremonial cleanness in handling the money than with the basic demands of justice for Jesus (Matt 27:3–10). Even after the crucifixion, death and burial of Jesus in the tomb of Joseph of Arimathea, they were so contemptuous of any possible resurrection-truth in the Man from Nazareth that they bribed the sentries of the tomb to keep silent about angels, earthquakes and stones rolled away from the tomb (Matt 28:11–15).

Men of violence

Lovers of money, inveterate plotters, scared of the people, scornful of the truth – these were some of the chief characteristics of those who wielded religious power at the time of Jesus. One other trait is obvious but needs pinpointing: they were given to violence. We know from contemporary (and earlier) records that the Pharisees were so zealous for their vision of a pure Judaism that on occasions they ruthlessly opposed their enemies (both real and imagined) by means of bribery, incarceration and execution. We see these violent methods nakedly employed in the growing conflict with Jesus – a classic example of the lethal combination provided by money, power and religion. Wealth, intrigue, fear, lies and violence were the five dominating forces at work among the religious leadership of first-century Palestine.

The conflict with Jesus

Jesus was intractably opposed to these forces and to the traditions, teaching and hypocrisy with which they were reinforced. But we can understand the full thrust of his opposition only by examining those ingredients in his ministry which chiefly provoked the wrath of the religious leadership. Such ingredients were fourfold: healing, deliverance from demons, forgiveness of sins and his claims for himself. The first three ingredients provoked from the people in general and from the religious leadership in particular two key questions: 'By what authority are you doing these things?' (Matt

21:23) and 'who is this?' (Luke 5:21; 7:49). In answering these two questions, either directly or indirectly, Jesus made such claims for himself as totally undermined the status and the authority of those who had held immense religious power. If Jesus truly was the Christ, the Son of God, and if he could therefore pronounce people forgiven, bring healing to the sick and set the demonised free, then indeed the kingdom of God had come upon them (cf. Matt 12:28) – the one thing the scribes and Pharisees, for all their knowledge and power, had not been able to achieve. They merely looked *forward* to the coming kingdom and the coming Christ: Jesus had brought in the kingdom.

We would, however, be mistaken if we understood the conflict between Jesus and the religious leadership of his day in remote theological terms. No doubt Jesus and the Pharisees disagreed theologically: the main difference, however, was in the impact of their different ministries. The Pharisees used religious power to impose burdens on people, to make them feel guilty, worthless and hopeless, to remove God from their reach, to leave them lost and weary. Jesus, moving in the power of the Holy Spirit, assured sinners (of all kinds) of forgiveness; brought healing to invalids, cripples, lepers and blind beggars; liberated those enslaved and destroyed by demons; and by these means brought people hope, joy, love and peace. The Pharisees locked people up in extremely narrow places; Jesus set them free to live and to enjoy living. The Pharisees concentrated on externals and trivia; Jesus went right to the heart and brought medicine to the soul. The Pharisees wanted to rule people's lives; Jesus came to be a servant and thereby to give people their freedom through his serving. The Pharisees imposed heavy burdens; Jesus carried people's burdens.

The perils of playing God

It was this blazing contrast between the imposition of religious power and the authority of divine servanthood which inevitably brought confrontation between the Pharisees and Jesus, culminating in his eventual elimination. The followers of Jesus are plainly commanded not to allow such self-assertive, dominating attitudes to creep into their lives: the command is unequivocally stated at the heart of the woes which Jesus sadly but angrily directs at the scribes and Pharisees in Matthew 23. These are his words to his disciples:

> But you are not to be called rabbi, for you have one teacher, and you are all brethren. And call no man your father on earth, for you have one Father, who is in heaven. Neither be called masters, for you have one master, the Christ. He who is greatest among you shall be your servant; whoever exalts himself will be humbled, and whoever humbles himself will be exalted (Matt 23:8–12).

Looking at these verses more closely, and looking at them in their context, one supreme and powerful truth shines out. God is our Father, Teacher and Lord/Master; true religious power is properly exercised when we behave towards one another on the pattern of God himself in Jesus – i.e. by becoming a servant, humbling ourselves and seeing true Christlikeness in terms of not-grasping, in pouring ourselves out for others.

As Father, God gives life. As Lord, Jesus requires and deserves our total allegiance. As Teacher, the Holy Spirit instructs us in the way we ought to go and, in particular, opens up to us the example and teaching of Jesus. No human being can bring life, spiritual life. No human being should command, let alone receive, our total allegiance. No human being has the authority to usurp the ministry of the Holy Spirit as our teacher (cf. 1 John 2:20, 27).

The behaviour of the scribes and Pharisees warns us, therefore, of the dangers of having a derived faith, not a direct faith; dependent discipleship, not a personal discipleship; a go-between or a guru to whom we go, rather than to God through Jesus by his Spirit. In the gospel of the kingdom of God I am given the privilege – and the responsibility – of letting Jesus by his Spirit sort me out, set me free, send me out: anything less than this is verging on or toying with Pharisaism. The Pharisees would not let Jesus get that close to them: such a personal, intimate, direct relationship with God was far too challenging and uncomfortable. They steadily

refused to repent, i.e. to admit they were wrong and to let
Jesus change them (cf. Luke 7:30). Instead, they used and
reinforced the religious system ('the traditions of the elders')
in order to bolster their own power and to justify their right to
play God with people's lives. Those who assume – or are
entrusted with – official (or unofficial) religious power today
must be specially sensitive to any tendency to play God in the
lives of others. The scribes and the Pharisees were doing it as a
habit. By such behaviour they indicated a culpable ignorance,
not merely of their own inner corruption and corruptibility,
but of the very nature of God himself. He is not a despot who
dominates, but a Saviour who stoops. We are indeed called to
imitate the Lord, not by playing God with the lives of others,
but by laying down our lives in humble service. True power –
religious or whatever – comes from such a lifestyle.

The following story can act as an illustration of this crucial
truth. However remote its setting may be from our own
experience, it holds up an uncomfortable mirror on our own
heart-attitudes:

At Benin City Airport, Nigeria, the jetliner was packed
with passengers. It had just begun to taxi toward the
runway. The pastor's Mercedes-Benz screeched to a halt in
front of the plane. The pastor jumped out and waved his
arms at the pilot. The plane stopped. The steps were
lowered. The captain stepped down and asked what the
pastor wanted.

'I have two of God's important servants who must go to
Lagos,' the pastor said. 'But we are loaded to capacity.
Every seat is full,' the captain explained. 'Never mind. Let
me on board. They all know me. Let me talk to them.'

The pastor mounted the steps, walked down the crowded
aisles . . . Suddenly he whirled around. 'Excuse me, my
friends. But I have two of God's special servants in my car.
They must go to Lagos today on this plane. Two of you will
get off now, so God's servants can board. God bless you.'

Then he pointed: 'You, get up. You can go tomorrow.'
Then to the other side he signalled: 'You, God bless you.
Get up. You can travel later.' Both obeyed, gathered their
belongings and followed the preacher from the plane.[4]

8 DON'T ROCK THE BOAT –
POLITICAL POWER

'The issue of power and the structure of power (who has power over whom and who can decide what for whom) are what we today call politics. In the time of Jesus politics was primarily a matter of who would be king.'[1] Because the essence of Jesus' message was the kingdom of God or the kingdom of heaven, his whole ministry was bound to be thoroughly political in its impact and implications. At key moments throughout those three years, the issue of 'who would be king' broke out into the open. But it was crystallised unmistakably in the events surrounding Jesus' arrest and trial, and culminating in his execution. The bulk of this chapter will therefore focus on the last twenty-four hours or so of his life, a period fully documented in each of the four gospels. Here 'we see Jesus no longer in the presence of religion, but of government'.[2]

Politics and the mission of Jesus

As we concentrate on the last twenty-four hours of Jesus' life, we need to remember that the specific theme of political power can properly be seen as the backdrop for virtually everything he said and did in those three years. If politics is indeed a matter of who has power over whom and who can decide what for whom, it is obvious that the whole mission of Jesus was inextricably bound up with such concerns. Jesus was part of the society of Israel, with its political tensions and power conflicts. In that volatile and violent situation, it is striking that his message contained neither a programme nor a strategy for political liberation. Yet that same message 'generated a dynamism of socio-political change – for his own time and for all history to come'.[3] It was only a few years after the death of Jesus in Jerusalem that opponents of his followers in Thessalonica (over a thousand miles away) were declaring: 'These men who have turned the world upside down have come here also . . . and they are all acting against the decrees of Caesar, saying that there is another king, Jesus' (Acts 17:6–7).

The incident in Thessalonica, part of the Roman province of Macedonia, pinpointed the direct conflict precipitated by Christians proclaiming Jesus as king in territory administered by a governor appointed by Caesar. This was precisely the charge levelled by the Sanhedrin against Jesus when he stood before Pontius Pilate, the governor of the Roman province of Judea: 'We found this man perverting our nation, and forbidding us to give tribute to Caesar, and saying that he himself is Christ a King' (Luke 23:2). There was, however, a significant difference between the two Roman provinces of Macedonia and Judea. In Macedonia there was only one recognised king, Caesar; in Judea, the unique interplay of Jewish religion and politics had led the pragmatic Romans to acknowledge the dynasty of the Herods as having local, but limited, authority. Thus, along with Pilate as Roman procurator, we read of Herod Antipas as a local king (in the region around Galilee) under the authority of Rome (cf. Luke 23:6–12). Only the southern part of the country, i.e. around Jerusalem, was permanently occupied by Roman soldiers. The middle and northern areas were under the client kingdoms of Herod Antipas and Archelaus – in the three years of Jesus' public ministry, therefore, he would have met different situations in Galilee and around Jerusalem.

The political implications

The political implications of Jesus' message and ministry worked, perforce, in two directions: challenging both the totalitarian rule of Rome and the more local authority of the Herods. His very birth in Bethlehem had aroused the fear and the fury of Herod the Great, as we saw earlier. Herod Antipas had acted true to family form, on at least one occasion deliberately attempting to eliminate Jesus: 'Some Pharisees came, and said to [Jesus], "Get away from here, for Herod wants to kill you"' (Luke 13:31) – which evoked Jesus' description of Herod as 'that fox' (Luke 13:32).

The role of Pontius Pilate

As for Pontius Pilate, contemporary secular sources tell us about three important incidents in his governorship of Judea, each of which illustrates the contempt and the fear which marked his attitude to the Jews.

On his first visit to Jerusalem, accompanied by a detachment of soldiers from the garrison of Caesarea, he deliberately ignored the practice of his predecessors, each of whom (in deference to Jewish sensitivities about graven images), before entering the holy city, had removed the little metal representation of the emperor attached to the top of the standards carried by the soldiers. Pilate was pursued by the Jews for several days, even back to his headquarters in Caesarea, but he refused to bow to their wishes. Eventually he surrounded the Jews in the local amphitheatre and threatened to kill them all unless they halted their demands. In response the Jews bared necks and offered them to the soldiers. Pilate climbed down, agreed that the metal images would in future be removed from the soldiers' standards, and spent the rest of his ten years in Palestine living down this political disaster.

The second incident might well have been prompted by Pilate's determination to improve the situation with the Jews. He wanted to develop the Jerusalem water-supply, a very necessary and valuable project. Pilate's political misjudgment was again to the fore, however, because he decided to raise the money required for his scheme by raiding the temple treasury – an action scarcely calculated to win popular, let alone priestly, support. The people started to rampage through the streets and Pilate's response was to send in plain-clothes soldiers, who at a given signal attacked the mob and killed many Jews – the Trojan horse tactic notoriously used in 1985 by the South African authorities on their own countrymen.

Pilate compounded his callous folly with a third disaster. He had special shields made, inscribed with the name of the emperor Tiberius, and placed them in the ancient palace of the Herods in Jerusalem. These votive shields were associated with the growing divinity cult which was emerging around the Roman emperor. Inevitably the fury of the Jews was once again aroused by such deliberate provocation, and they actually reported the matter to Tiberius, who ordered Pilate to remove the shields.

This last incident underlines the vulnerability of Pilate as *praefectus* of Judea. Pilate's whole career was in jeopardy as a result of the Jewish report placed in the hands of the emperor. It is clear that he must have been walking a tightrope throughout his ten years in the province. To have been put in charge of such a notoriously unruly part of the Roman Empire, Pilate must have been a hardliner, with a proven track-record as an army officer. He was used to employing strong-arm tactics, but in many ways any prefect of Judea knew that he was on a hiding to nothing. His was an extremely lucrative posting, especially as compared with his salary as an army officer, but it was fraught with potential for disgrace and disaster.

None of these drawbacks should, however, blind us to the immense power which Pilate possessed as governor of Judea. He was responsible for defence, civil administration and the financial management of the province. Internal affairs, mainly connected with the Mosaic law, were the responsibility of the Sanhedrin. Historically this had included the right to inflict capital punishment. But this right was withdrawn and now it belonged to the Roman governor, as in every part of the empire. In such a volatile province as Judea, the Roman government would not, in any case, have allowed the local authorities to retain such crucial power. If the Sanhedrin, in the case of the blasphemy charge initially brought against Jesus, wanted to proceed to execution, they were bound to introduce more clearly political accusations. Only then would Pilate (the Pilate they had come to know over the years) have responded to their determined pleas to have Jesus put to death.

A classic confrontation

These details about Pontius Pilate help us better to appreciate the dynamics of this remarkable encounter between the most powerful man in the land and a young carpenter-turned-preacher in the last few hours of his life. This is the classic confrontation between the man who represented total, if not totalitarian, human power and the man who represented a completely new quality of power, the power of God. It is worth repeating that in the Judea of his time the ministry and the message of Jesus were bound to bring him on to collision-course with the religious authorities and – given the political realities of occupied Palestine – therefore into confrontation with imperial Rome. Nevertheless, it requires massive special pleading to see in Jesus a revolutionary leader against Rome. There were plenty of Zealots around, who were overtly and violently into freedom-fighting: Barabbas was probably a Zealot; Simon, one of the disciples of Jesus, certainly had been a Zealot; Judas Iscariot at least had strong sympathies, if not active involvement. It has been argued that James and John ('the sons of thunder') and even Simon Peter all had Zealot leanings.[4] When the time came – at his arrest and trial – for Jesus to face the powers that be in Caiaphas, Herod and Pilate, he made a point of manifestly rejecting the Zealot option, and he did so more than once.

In other words, however politically provocative and suspect his teaching and behaviour, Jesus was pursuing a greater goal – the kingdom of God. As we have seen, the very terminology of kings and kingdoms was like dynamite in that political situation. Jesus neither trimmed down his message to accommodate these dangers nor dramatised it to provoke violence. He pursued his God-given calling to its fulfilment, taking in his stride the inevitable flak, and using every opportunity to make the issues of the kingdom of God plain to those who crossed his path. In this sense his behaviour towards Pilate was no different from his behaviour at less climactic moments of his career. He simply did and said what he believed to be right . . . and took the consequences.

The net result of this consistent loyalty to a higher vocation, epitomised in his encounter with Pilate, was that the kingdom of God was indeed manifested in his life, suffering and death. In addition, Pilate (like everyone else he encountered) was compelled (directly and indirectly) to face up to the responsibilities involved in holding political power – not simply *vis-à-vis* the sovereignty of the emperor, but in the more ultimate sense of answerability for his use/abuse of power to God himself. These two achievement of Jesus – proclaiming God's kingdom and underlining human accountability to God for the exercise of power – may turn out still to be the main calling of the disciples of Jesus in any setting of political power.

Such a conclusion is borne out by one of the most fascinating and instructive incidents in the life of Paul. Again in Jerusalem, he was brought before Felix, the Roman governor – a man who 'exercised the power of a king with the disposition of a slave' and, 'backed by vast influence, believed himself free to commit any crime'.[5] With such a venal and violent governor Paul spoke frequently about faith in Jesus Christ, a subject which greatly alarmed Felix, presumably because, Luke tells us (Acts 24:25), the topics covered were 'justice and self-control and future judgment' – a trio of themes not on the top of the governor's agenda, but central to Paul's message concerning the kingdom of God initiated by Jesus of Nazareth.

As we now examine the gospel accounts of the encounter between Jesus and Pilate, these (and many other) perspectives will become more apparent. According to John (the fullest account of the encounter between the two men), Jesus spoke directly to Pilate on only four occasions, each of which was full of searching significance. The first three remarks all occurred in what is recorded as a single conversation; but it is worth examining them point by point.

Perhaps the problem will go away

When Pilate initially asked Jesus the leading question, 'Are you the King of the Jews?' (John 18:33), Jesus replied: 'Do you say this of your own accord, or did others say it to you about me?' (John 18:34). The issue of kingship (who has power over whom) was, as we have already noted, a contemporary political issue of immense significance, and was at the core of Jesus' rejection by the Jewish hierarchy. Did Pilate want to know whether Jesus was leading a Jewish revolution against Rome? Or had Pilate simply been coached by the chief priests? The answer to Pilate's question depended on the governor's answer to this enquiry from Jesus – it would be 'No' to the first possibility, 'Yes' to being the messianic king of Israel.

In addition, it is possible that Jesus wanted to establish the degree to which Pilate had truly understood his message concerning the sovereign claims of the kingdom of God. Was the governor genuinely intent on discovering the truth about his claims? Or was he merely going along with the prejudices of the Jewish hierarchy? We cannot tell; but we can deduce one or two possibilities from the vehemence of Pilate's retort: 'Am I a Jew? Your own nation and the chief priests have handed you over to me' (John 18:35).

Pilate was not at all prepared to get drawn into personal discussions on matters involving Jewish controversy. He utterly despised the Jews, as had been sadly demonstrated by his actions since becoming governor, and he would never admit to being personally involved in their petty squabbles. As far as Pilate was concerned, let the Jews confine themselves to their religious intricacies, and let the Roman authorities look after matters political.

At that stage he presumably hoped that there was nothing of genuinely political significance in the Jewish fury against Jesus. According to Luke he was soon disabused of such a vain hope, because the political *savoir-faire* of the chief priests cleverly unearthed at least four charges, sufficiently political to make even Pilate's hair stand on end: 'We found this man perverting our nation, and forbidding us to give tribute to Caesar, and saying that he himself is Christ a King . . . He stirs up the people, teaching throughout all Judea, from Galilee even to this place' (Luke 23:2, 5). Then Pilate knew that his hopes for a speedy return to the quiet life in Caesarea had been well and truly stymied. He was face to face with a man and a situation with the potential to bring all his moral weaknesses and political gaffes home to roost.

Keep religion and politics separate

The Nazarene's next statement left Pilate completely lost. When he asked Jesus directly, 'What have you done', Jesus took the conversation straight back to the matter of kingship: 'My kingship is not of this world; if my kingship were of this world, my servants would fight, that I might not be handed over to the Jews; but my kingship is not from the world' (John 18:36). The Jewish leaders, hoping desperately for a powerful king to oust the Romans, might be completely unable to see in Jesus their true king. The Roman governor, intent on keeping the peace as a loyal representative of the all-powerful emperor of Rome, might find any talk of kingship highly provocative and even seditious. But Jesus had no intention of softening his message or his claims – 'I have a kingdom . . .'

It is a great pity that most English translations of this crucial statement by Jesus about his kingship obscure its true meaning. Serious misunderstandings have produced not just inbuilt non-involvement in politics but passionate opposition to any proper involvement by any followers of Jesus. These all revolve around the two-letter word 'of'. Three times in the Revised Standard Version (for example), as quoted above, Jesus apparently asserts that his kingdom, God's kingdom, has nothing to do with 'this world': it is 'not of this world . . . not of this world, not from the world'. Could anything, say the pietists, be any clearer? Christians obviously cannot and should not get involved in politics: let the Church look after spiritual matters, and leave politics to the politicians.

The Greek preposition at issue here is *ek*, which has the very precise and consistent meaning of 'proceeding from' – i.e. indicating source and origin. It occurs twice in the verse, but is not actually used in the final phrase of Jesus' statement. The Greek word used at the end of the verse is even more explicit: *enteuthen* is an adverbial phrase meaning 'from here', again stressing source and origin. Jesus was saying, therefore, 'My kingship does not have its source and its origin in this world . . . My kingly authority does not proceed from here at all.' The word translated (in the RSV) 'kingship', *basileia*, means something like 'the kingly sway I exercise' –

referring to the actual authority which Jesus possessed and expressed.

In other words, Jesus was saying to Pilate (with increasing clarity), 'I *am* a king: I possess kingly power . . . But I do not get that power from anywhere in this world: from the Sanhedrin, from my followers, from my money, from my education or my knowledge, from the Roman emperor. I receive my power and my authority, my royal dominion, from somewhere else and some*one* else entirely.' Jesus was making no statement at all about the arena in which his kingly power operated, only about its origin. The whole thrust of his message and ministry made it unmistakably and irrefutably plain that his kingly rule was being – and was to be – exercised over every square-inch of this world: over every government and nation; over every community and family; over every man, woman and child in every generation. This is why Leon Morris, for example, clouds the issue when he comments (on John 18:36), 'It [Jesus' kingdom] does not take its origin from this world, and it is not basically concerned with this world.'[6] He is correct in his first comment; he is wrong in his second comment.

Violence: a non-option

Because the kingly power and rule of Jesus did not have their origins in any thing or anyone limited to *this* world, there followed one fundamental fact about the way it operated. Unlike any worldly government, such as the Sanhedrin and the Roman governor, the officers or ministers of Jesus' kingdom had no right to resort to force or violence, to 'fight'. Indeed the implication of Jesus' words are that once they do 'fight' they have forfeited their authority and power. The Sanhedrin had used soldiers to arrest Jesus; Pontius Pilate needed soldiers to keep the turbulent province of Judea under control. To establish and to spread his kingly rule, Jesus needed no soldiers, no force, no violence, no fighting – indeed, he renounced them all. Had he not commanded Peter to sheath his sword when on the point of being arrested? His words on that occasion had been uncompromising: 'all who take the sword will perish by the sword. Do you think that I cannot appeal to my Father, and he will at once send me twelve legions of angels?' (Matt 26:52–53).

Theoretically, Jesus could have resorted to the power of violence to prevent his arrest and execution. His refusal to do so not only stopped him flouting the eternal purpose which the Father and the Son had been pursuing; it also prevented what would have been an equally devastating betrayal – the Son of God stooping, at the crunch, to the methods of disobedient, rebellious humanity. His followers, especially Peter, had not been able to appreciate the essential dynamics of the kingdom of God. Jesus had needed to stop them operating with worldly power. But there, face to face with the representative of total worldly power, Jesus intended to make it plain for all time that *his* officers do not fight.

Still today, Jesus is concerned to impress on his followers the radical contrast between *his* kingdom and the kingdoms of this world. He did not – let it be noticed – strip either the governor or the Sanhedrin of the right to use worldly force and power. He simply spelt out that for him and his followers there was another way, another kingdom, another power. Whatever the threats, whatever the perils, whatever the stakes, whatever the temptations, Jesus proclaimed the kingdom of God. The source of the kingdom's power must mould the methods used by the kingdom's citizens. So, far from the end justifying the means, he who is the beginning and the end must dictate the means, must master the men and women he has called to follow him.

Don't confuse me with the truth

This important perspective is taken one step further in the final part of this seminal conversation between Pilate and Jesus. The governor assumes, however vaguely, that Jesus is a king of some kind and therefore someone who presents a substantial threat to the sovereignty of Caesar and to his own authority: 'So you are a king?' he says. Instead of giving him an unequivocal affirmative, Jesus then introduces a dimension which takes the initiative completely out of Pilate's hands. He replies: 'You say that I am a king. For this I was born, and for this I have come into the world, to bear witness to the truth' (John 18:37).

Pilate's reaction to 'the truth' has been variously interpreted. Even if he would not stay for an answer to his ageless question 'What is truth?' (John 18:38), this was certainly not a 'jesting Pilate'. Those in power have learnt over the years to be extremely chary of truth – or, at best, to be 'economical with the truth'. Because politics is basically the art of the possible, expediency has always triumphed over ethics; and expediency, unlike ethics, does not like to deal in matters of truth and falsehood. Its vocabulary harps on words like wise and unwise, appropriate and inappropriate, reasonable and unreasonable, practicable and impracticable. Truth sharpens the focus, introduces black and white into a vista of greys, compels us to come down on one side or the other.

Because Pilate was unable to face up to the truth in what Jesus had said and in his very Person, he proceeded to act in ways which have classically characterised those who reject the truth. For example, his next step was to find a way of releasing Jesus which would placate the Jewish leaders: 'you have a custom that I should release one man for you at the Passover' (John 18:39). Instead of facing up to the truth about Jesus, as witnessed in his own conviction – 'I find no crime in him' (a judgment he states twice, John 18:38; 19:4) – Pilate avoided the implications of Jesus' innocence in order to please the Jews. He ought, in the interests of truth, simply to have acquitted Jesus. But he wanted to 'satisfy the crowd' (Mark 15:15). Whenever popular approval dominates, truth is the first casualty.

I must find a way out of this

Rather than face up to the truth in Jesus, Pilate continued to look for a way out, even to the extent of attempting to get the Jewish leaders to transcend their own legitimate authority: 'Take him yourselves and crucify him' (John 19:6). That dangerously foolish riposte led to a moment of supreme truth: 'We have a law, and by that law he ought to die, because he has made himself the Son of God' (John 19:7). Pilate would have been as confused about the notion of God having a son as any orthodox Jew. His own religious background would not have been of much help to him in his confusion. Already about to sink into a morass of perilous impotence, the Roman governor now had to confront the possibility that he might be on the verge of crucifying 'the Son of God', whatever that might mean. However pragmatically pagan this Roman might have been, such a spectre would have made an already vulnerable man even more panicky. John's own comment is: 'When Pilate heard these words, he was the more afraid' (John 19:8). Where did this carpenter from Nazareth truly come from? The truth was too big to contemplate.

At least, thought Pilate, I can get him to speak to me. But Jesus refused to speak to him – and there are few things more threatening to those in authority than silent prisoners. Two of the most well-known twentieth-century practitioners of non-violent resistance (of the kind typified by Jesus' silence before Pilate) were Mahatma Gandhi and Martin Luther King. Gandhi's principle was that of *satyagraha*, or force which is born of truth and love (or non-violence). King wrote, 'Non-violence has a way of disarming the opponent. It exposes his moral defences, it weakens his morale and at the same time works on his conscience. He just doesn't know how to handle it.'[7] When the truth has been clearly spoken, as it had by Jesus to Pilate, there is nothing more to be said unless the truth has been received, acknowledged and pursued. This Pilate had signally failed to do; instead, he had chased as many avenues of evasion as possible. Jesus refused to speak to him . . . and when Jesus has nothing more to say to anyone, he is in dire peril.

The blustering of a frightened man

Pilate then took refuge in blustering, threats and swinging rank: 'Do you not know that I have power to release you, and power to crucify you?' (John 19:10). In effect, Pilate was telling Jesus, 'Don't you realise who I am? I'm the governor. I represent Caesar, Rome, the empire. I possess total authority. Who do you think you are?' The reply of Jesus to this empty bravado provides the perfect and permanent commentary on all human power: 'You would have no power over me unless it had been given you from above' (John 19:11). This statement needs to be read in conjunction with Jesus' earlier remark: 'My kingship is not from the world' (John 18:36). In these two comments, Jesus establishes the source and the origin both of his own power and of Pilate's power – both come from God, the one being exercised appropriately and truthfully, the other being exercised selfishly, ambivalently and arrogantly.

Pilate acknowledged that his power was derived from Caesar, but he could not see further than Rome. Jesus wanted to emphasise that even the totalitarian authority of Caesar was a derived authority, derived and delegated from almighty God. He had already stressed that, in exercising such power from God, neither he nor his disciples would resort to force. To Pilate he now stresses that, inasmuch as the governor's power was derived from God, it must be exercised in accordance with the truth, not with either popular demands or personal ambition. The crunch was Pilate's desire to live up to his position as 'Caesar's friend' (John 19:12). This phrase described a special 'in-group' with considerable influence at Rome, into which Pilate had been introduced by marriage. His wife moved in all the right circles and Pilate presumably prized both her knowledge and his own derived status. With sinister accuracy the Jewish leaders played on this fact – so cleverly, indeed, that he was prepared to ignore the urgent pleas of his wife, when she urged him to 'Have nothing to do with that righteous man' (Matt 27:19).

Listen to your wife

Even the truth contained in his wife's vivid dream (constantly in the scriptures a means for receiving a message from God) could not divert Pilate from his shuffling departure from the truth. Try as he might, he could not convince himself, Jesus or anyone else that he was innocent of 'this man's blood' (Matt

27:24). No public washing of his hands could cleanse away his falsehood. No petulant refusal to change his mind about the *titulus* over the cross of Jesus ('What I have written I have written,' John 19:22) could obscure his dereliction of duty in condemning to death an innocent man. No subsequent gesture of magnanimity to Joseph of Arimathea, who wanted to provide a decent burial for the corpse of Jesus, could justify his treatment of the living body of Jesus by scourging and by crucifixion. In one sense, Jesus was to Pilate like any number of Jews who caused serious trouble and were executed by the Romans. In another sense – as the gospel narratives (especially John's) make plain – Jesus was totally different from the usual Jewish revolutionary.

Pilate had walked all over the truth, as it had been borne witness to in the words, demeanour and very person of Jesus. No doubt there are many further nuances to the encounter between these two men. What is clear is that the inherent power and authority of the truth in Jesus had been brought forcibly to bear on this wielder of supreme political power. Because Pilate chose to ignore, and ultimately to reject, the truth, he inexorably moved towards the place where he could exercise his considerable authority only in fear, falsehood and folly.

In a deeper sense than he realised, Pilate actually offered the Jewish people (egged on by their leaders) a straight choice between the two personifications of worldly power and divine power under his control: Jesus Barabbas, the freedom-fighter on behalf of his country, due to be executed for insurrection and murder; Jesus Christ, the Prince of peace, framed for insurrection, but due to be executed in order that he might win true and full freedom on behalf of the whole human race. 'Whom do you want me to release for you,' asked Pilate, 'Jesus Barabbas or Jesus who is called Christ?' (Matt 27:17). Pilate posed the same question twice . . . and the ordinary people, instigated by leaders with a lot to lose if Jesus' pattern of power prevailed, opted for the way of 'smash and grab', not the way of serve and give.

So Pilate listened to the Jewish crowds, not to the King of the Jews: 'their voices prevailed' (Luke 23:23). Pilate knew the truth; he knew the right thing to do; he knew what he ought to do; he knew the extent – and, eventually, the true origin – of his personal power . . . but he walked away from it all. Christians together state their belief: 'He suffered under Pontius Pilate'. Jesus, the one in whom God had invested supreme power, willingly submitted himself to the whims and weaknesses of the one individual who – in that time and place – represented virtually complete human power and authority.

The loneliness of leadership

This encounter between Pilate and Jesus underlines the extreme loneliness of those who exercise worldly power. One of the formidable dissuaders, especially in today's increasingly egalitarian world, affecting anyone considering a position of power is this apparently inevitable isolation from one's contemporaries. In schools and colleges in the 1970s, this fear of loneliness fostered widespread refusal to accept positions of leadership. Many people in all walks of life still reject any promotion for similar reasons.

So Pilate found any genuine friendship in Palestine to be impossible. By his very status as 'Caesar's friend', he was ostracised from any peer-group relationship with either Jew or Roman. There is something slightly sad about the comment of Luke on Pilate's relationship with Herod Antipas, which was reversed in their common rejection (and fear) of the truth in Jesus: 'That day Herod and Pilate became friends – before this they had been enemies' (Luke 23:12 NIV). Jesus was, in effect, offering Pilate the understanding and directness of a true friend. Such a gift is arguably the most valuable possession anyone in power can receive.

Although details cannot, for obvious reasons, be divulged, more and more Christians in positions of considerable authority are today finding the strength which comes from such Christ-inspired and Christ-centred friendship. I think, for example, of a powerful businessman who regularly spends three or four days alone with a very nondescript, unremarkable Christian friend who has no worldly power whatever. Those times are spent in sober assessment and frank sharing.

Pilate, by contrast, had become isolated in his immense

responsibilities – an isolation which a notoriously unpredictable Herod Antipas was hardly equipped or eager to relieve.
'There is no worse solitude than that of the powerful.'[8]

The use of force

What do the attitudes and actions of Jesus towards Pilate have
to say about the use of force and violence by those with
positions or opportunities of power – either the violence of
repressive governments or revolutionary violence? Is violence ever justifiable as a specifically Christian option? What
seems clear is that the followers of Jesus, acting and speaking
explicitly in his name as the Christian church, are not free to
espouse any violent expression of power. Such a stance, it
appears to me, is distinct from what may be the legitimate
use of power by a government, or by those fighting what
theologians have come to call 'a just war'.

According to St Paul, there is a proper use of 'the sword' by
those in authority in punishing evildoers, as a deterrent and as
a back-up to commending good behaviour (cf. Rom 13:1–5).
Those who thus exercise authority in a nation are under a
solemn, indeed a godly, obligation to uphold justice and to
recognise their authority as having been delegated from God.
When these boundaries are regularly crossed, revolutionary
violence is inevitably spawned – as is classically the case in
South Africa today. In such a situation, people like Desmond
Tutu will find themselves, as disciples of Jesus, committed to
non-violence, but also caught up precariously in the crossfire
between violent men in authority and violent men in revolution. This has meant walking into a lynch-mob of thousands
to rescue a man, accused of being a government stooge, from
death by 'necklacing'.[9]

Such a stance seems to take its cue directly from the
example of Jesus, who refused to condone (let alone to
embrace) either the repressive violence of the authorities
(Jewish or Roman) or the revolutionary violence of the
Zealots. Instead, he allowed it all to be directed at himself, to
the point where he was destroyed – only to rise triumphantly
from the grave. His disciples in any generation can hardly act

differently and still claim to be expressing the mind and the example of Christ.

It is, nevertheless, conceivable that an individual Christian can properly maintain his or her commitment to Christ as Lord, while endorsing in the political arena policies and practices which fall short of Christ's way, but which offer the lesser of two evils. What in such circumstances ought not to be done is to claim such a stance as a *Christian* stance, i.e. one which reflects the way of Jesus Christ.

Secular power and the powers of darkness

So far, we have concentrated on the interpersonal encounter between Jesus and Pilate, examining it at the level of the Son of God face to face with the most powerful person in the nation. But there was more, far more, to this encounter than the meeting of two significant people. Jesus made that plain when, at the point of his arrest, he said to the chief priests and officers of the temple and elders, 'this is your hour, and the power of darkness' (Luke 22:53) – a comment brought dramatically to the forefront within twenty-four hours, when darkness covered the land in the middle of the day as he hung dying on the cross.

It is not fanciful, therefore, to see the spiritual powers of darkness viciously and desperately at work in the last hours of Jesus' life. The same pressures which Satan had originally brought to bear on Jesus in the power struggle in the wilderness, were now hurled at him in those last hours. Representatives of human, worldly power were able to achieve their own ends; but Jesus was clear in his own mind that they were instruments (however responsible for their own actions) of a greater power.

Some years later, Paul consistently interpreted the climax to Jesus' ministry from this perspective. In writing to Christians at Colossae, for example, about the impact on believers of the death of Christ, he concluded: 'He disarmed the principalities and powers and made a public example of them, triumphing over them in it [the cross]' (Col 2:15). Again, in the passage in Philippians 2, which we have argued to be so central to our understanding of Jesus and power, Paul stresses the self-humbling and obedience which brought him to a place of triumph over every such spiritual (and human) power.

In his important book *The Politics of Jesus* John Howard Yoder, in a careful study of Christ and these powers, presents the following analysis:

> . . . the Powers cannot simply be destroyed or set aside or ignored. Their sovereignty must be broken. This is what Jesus did, concretely and historically, by living among men a genuinely free and human existence. This life brought him, as any genuinely human existence will bring any man, to the cross. In his death the Powers – in this case the most worthy, weighty representatives of Jewish religion and Roman politics – acted in collusion. Like all men, he too was subject (but in his case quite willingly) to these powers . . . Therefore his cross is a victory . . . Here we have for the first time to do with a man who is not the slave of any power . . . Not even to save his own life will he let himself be made a slave of these Powers.[10]

Yoder's last remark points to the paradoxical significance of the cross. By not going along with the methods and the assumptions of those who wielded immense earthly power, Jesus set himself apart from them. More than that, he humbled himself and became submissive to their power in obedience to his Father. By so doing he rendered them impotent, for all their impressiveness and bravado. This is plain in the narratives which we have already examined, where Jesus and Pilate are in confrontation. When the writers of the New Testament described spiritual powers at work in and through those who exercise worldly power, they were not being superstitious or naive. They were communicating truths unapparent to purely human reasoning, but continually operative in the life and death of Jesus, as well as subsequently in the lives of his disciples. To be involved in exercising any kind of power in today's world, but to remain ignorant or sceptical of these spiritual factors, is to run the risk of being blind both to the true ingredients of human power and to the radical contrast afforded by Jesus' power.

This perspective is not – as some would suggest – a foolish plunge into obscurantism. The writers of the New Testament never presented the spiritual conflict in terms of some magic rigmarole. As Yoder states, 'the Powers have been defeated, not by some kind of cosmic hocus-pocus, but by the concreteness of the cross'.[11] No wonder Jesus was so direct and uncompromising with anyone, especially his closest friends, who tried to divert him from the cross. Only by holding firm to the way of the cross could he finally destroy all the spiritual powers which hold men and women in bondage, and which concentrate their impact on individuals (such as Herod, Caiaphas and Pilate) and institutions (such as the Sanhedrin) with the greatest worldly power.

There is one corollary of overriding importance for Christians who want to see Jesus Christ acknowledged as Lord of communities and nations. The way of Jesus is most accurately followed by those who do not try to manipulate the power structures of the world for Christian ends, but who deliberately and consistently challenge those structures with the radically different values and priorities of Jesus – the one who 'came not to be served but to serve' (Mark 10:45). Yoder, for example, urges us to reject the assumption that 'the forces which really determine the march of history are in the hands of the leaders of the armies and the markets'.[12] Equally, he challenges the belief (prevalent among Christians who want to make a national or international impact) that Christians 'will need to seek, like everyone else – in fact, in competition with everyone else – to become in their turn the lords of the state and the economy, so as to use that power toward the ends they consider desirable'.[13] The way of Jesus is too radical to be fitted into the mould shaped by any human exercise of power. He has broken the mould and wants his followers to do the same, not snatching and dominating, but serving and giving.

9   VICTORY AND FREEDOM –
RESURRECTION POWER

We cannot read the description of the early Christian church, from Acts through the epistles to Revelation, without being immediately and forcefully struck by the sheer dynamism which took hold of those first Christians from Pentecost onwards. This was, after all, precisely what Jesus himself had promised before he returned to his Father in heaven: 'stay in the city until you have been clothed with power from on high' (Luke 24:49 NIV) – reiterated in Acts 1:8, 'you will receive power when the Holy Spirit comes on you'. In both cases this power is to equip the disciples to be witnesses to Jesus, to tell others what they have seen and heard in Jesus.

If there is any consistency or logic in the ministry of Jesus thus entrusted to his disciples, we expect the characteristics of Jesus' earthly ministry during those three packed and vivid years to be manifested in the disciples by the Holy Spirit within them. If, then, the previous chapters of this book have with any accuracy portrayed the characteristics of Jesus' ministry, notably in connection with the theme of power, then we anticipate that the same truths will shine out of the early church. In particular, we would expect the first Christians, in so far as they were faithfully imitating Jesus, to show their true greatness in not chasing after or grasping power, but in pouring themselves out for others and humbling themselves to serve one another and their own generation.

Bigger and better?

But, it will be said (loudly by some and quietly by others), does not the resurrection change all that? Do Christians not live on the other side of the cross? Paul, after all, wrote about God's 'incomparably great power in us who believe'. To what can we liken such power? Do we have any criterion for evaluating it? Yes, says Paul, 'That power is like the working of his mighty strength, which he exerted in Christ when he raised him from the dead and seated him at his right hand' (Eph 1:19–20 NIV). Resurrection power is, therefore, the power of God to raise men and women from the dead; and our model and precedent is the resurrection of Jesus from the tomb of Joseph of Arimathea on the first Easter morning, inextricably coupled with his ascension to the place of supreme authority at God's right hand. The only natural conclusion we can draw is that such a demonstration of power transcends all other demonstrations of power at any time or anywhere or by anyone. This power is greater even than the power unleashed by a massive nuclear explosion – i.e. it surpasses even the potential in nuclear power to destroy the earth as we know it. This fact Paul, however unconsciously, asserts when he describes the resurrection/ascension power operative in Jesus as 'far above all rule and authority, power and dominion' (Eph 1:21).

The question must still be asked: in what does this transcendent power consist? Our language suggests strongly that such power is greater, more effective than any other: as Paul puts it, this power is 'far above' all other power. We automatically assume that it is human power to the nth degree; if nuclear power is super-power, resurrection power is hyper-power.

Our understanding of God's power, through the resurrection and ascension of Jesus, is thereby produced solely in terms of *comparison*. What if the ministry of Jesus, which must remain our model, is intended to draw a vivid, indeed a total, *contrast* between human power and divine power? Perhaps the resurrection and ascension of Jesus do not indicate transcendence so much as displacement and replacement: a whole new world has been generated – its character and qualities were sketched out in the life and death of Jesus; its reality has burst into our existence in the resurrection and ascension of Jesus. In particular, the Holy Spirit brings substantial and increasing glimpses of this new world, as he goes to work in Christian believers to produce the very life of Jesus in our mortal bodies. For this to happen, the old must be displaced and be replaced with the new. As far as power is concerned, worldly and human expressions of power must be displaced and replaced with the power characteristic of Jesus. This will mean rejecting any credal statement which introduces a false triumphalism into our faith. Commenting on this tendency in the church in Latin America since the sixteenth century, Georges Casalis observes that the primitive church's profession of faith, 'Jesus is Lord' meant that 'Jesus, who is the victorious servant, was turned into a heavenly emperor, which means exactly the opposite'.[1]

A complete contrast

For Paul, this sheer contrast between human power and divine power as demonstrated in Jesus is specifically pinpointed in the cross. Here the man who was God emptied himself, humbled himself, poured himself out – the classic example, by human yardsticks, of utter weakness. To see in such an event any possible source of salvation for the sin-sick human race is crass foolishness. By any human criterion the cross of Jesus is the very antithesis of power. The message of the cross is foolishness (1 Cor 1:18).

But, proclaims Paul, this same message turns out to be immensely powerful for those who have their eyes opened to appreciate what was actually happening (1 Cor 1:18). There, in the act and fact of Jesus being put to death on a cross, the power of God was being demonstrated. Christ is the power of God (1 Cor 1:24). In that demonstration of supreme human weakness we see the very power of God – not in the reversal of the cross by his resurrection, but in the reinforcement by the cross of this central truth: Jesus saw true God-ness in terms of not grasping for himself, but of giving himself. That is true power, the power of God – in total contrast to all human power. By raising Jesus from the dead, God fully vindicated that kind of power. This self-denying, self-giving lifestyle contains within it the power of God.

A number of derivative truths spring from this understanding of the cross and Paul from time to time expounds them.

For example, if the unvarnished weakness of Jesus crucified perfectly portrays the power of God, the message of the cross must not be obscured with 'words of human wisdom' – rhetoric can empty the cross of Christ of its power, because it attempts to describe weakness in words which signify human strength through their wisdom and articulacy. Let fine preachers beware: the stark simplicity of God's power in human weakness at the cross must not be covered up with human brilliance.

By adopting such a self-denying attitude to his proclamation of Jesus, Paul ensured that his preaching was in 'demonstration of the Spirit's power' (1 Cor 2:4). The power of the Spirit brings home to ready listeners the power of God in the cross of Jesus. As they respond in faith, they discover this message is good news; it brings salvation. So Paul is certainly not ashamed of such a message (Rom 1:16). By boldly proclaiming it in an unadorned manner, he in fact ensured that the faith his listeners then exercised was genuinely resting in God's power demonstrated in the cross, not in any brilliant presentation by himself (1 Cor 2:4–5).

A challenge to achievers

Now Paul was a proud, resourceful, able and successful man. He was, in today's terms, an achiever. That is why the gospel of Jesus cut him so painfully down to size. Any impartial reading of his experiences as an apostle brings the conclusion that he was forced to endure almost unparalleled suffering and deprivation. Each and every one of these circumstances compelled him to taste his frailty, vulnerability, mortality and weakness. In the face of all these sufferings, he learnt not merely to endure but to rejoice, even to boast, about them. Why? Because God had made it plain to him over the years that 'My . . . power is made perfect in weakness'. Paul decided as a result: 'Therefore I will boast all the more gladly about my weaknesses, so that Christ's power may rest on me' (2 Cor 12:9 NIV).

God wanted his own power, revealed in giving and serving, to be demonstrated as fully as possible in Paul's life. Paul's own understanding of power had been nurtured by the privileges of his Roman citizenship (Acts 16:37; 22:25–30), the pedigree of his family background (Phil 3:5), the purity of his religious fervour (Phil 3:6) and the assets of his fine education (Acts 22:3). He came to see all these as so much garbage, when contrasted with being in Christ and knowing Christ in the power of his resurrection and in the fellowship of his sufferings (Phil 3:4b–11). Through coming to know Christ better in suffering, he came to know also the power of his resurrection. But to do that Paul knew he needed to be weak and to taste his weakness: by his resurrection power Jesus gradually wrote the true power of God in Paul. At the end of that most revealing of all his letters, 2 Corinthians, Paul writes: 'He [Christ] is not weak in dealing with you, but is powerful among you . . . Likewise, we are weak in him, yet by God's power we will live with him to serve you' (2 Cor 13:3–4 NIV). 'By God's power we will live with Jesus to serve . . .' – so the resurrection power of Jesus is given to train us to be servants, to be like him, to imitate him.

Convincing the world

There is, actually, no other way for the unbelieving world to recognise the complete contrast between human power and God's power. Unless they can see obviously weak and fragile human beings manifestly demonstrating a superhuman freedom to serve and to give, they will never understand the power of God in the cross of Christ.

This understanding of the death and resurrection of Jesus has an immensely significant bearing on the agony of Latin America today. Reflecting on the way the cross and the resurrection have been traditionally portrayed on that continent since the *conquistadores*, Saúl Trinidad passionately laments the fact that 'The Christ of the cross, of the death that conquers . . . "has become the archetypical beggar, some sort of scarecrow, a footstool for the feet of everybody, a compendium of miseries and a sampler of humiliations".'[2] 'As for the Christ of the resurrection', continues Trinidad, '. . . they have made of him a heavenly monarch, the guarantor of his lieutenants and vicars, the kings of earth, and the oppressors who bear the title "benefactor".'[3] This lament helps us to see what can happen when one version of the cross is backed up by another version of the resurrection, without any consistent thread between the two: the status quo of injustice and oppression is given religious sanction.

So long as Christians see their task as to be strong, self-sufficient, in command and successful, the unbelieving world will assume that God is really interested only in people who have it all together. They will also continue in the comfortable myth that God helps those who help themselves, with its lethal assumption that, if we do our best, God will be pleased with us and usher us into heaven when we die.

The good news of Jesus is rather different. A world based on human power is under divine judgment; Jesus has shown us the way of divine power in self-emptying and servanthood; through his death and resurrection, he has brought to birth a totally new world, in which 'It is more blessed to give than to receive' (Acts 20:35). By his Holy Spirit he expresses this divine power in the lives of those who receive Jesus as Lord. We have this priceless treasure in pots of clay (i.e. our fragile human bodies), 'to show that this all-surpassing power is from God and not from us' (2 Cor 4:7 NIV).

> The reason why the cross is a victory is that it has opened a breach, once for all, in the prison wall of the selfish will to power. From henceforth and forever it shall be clear that only those who refuse to hold onto life for themselves can enable others to live.[4]

The power to change lives

Nothing so far explained in this chapter should detract from the immense impact which this kind of power will have in our lives. It will, for example, provide the inner impetus to turn away from sexual immorality: 'The body is not meant for sexual immorality, but for the Lord, and the Lord for the body. By his power God raised the Lord from the dead, and he will raise us also' (1 Cor 6:13–14 NIV). The implication of this statement is that God's power, resurrection power, lifts us out of both physical death and the kind of spiritual death produced by self-indulgence, not self-denial, in our sexuality.

What is true in the area of our sexuality holds good in the face of all kinds of temptation: we may have an external 'form of godliness' (2 Tim 3:5 NIV), but in practice deny the true power of God which alone can make us like Jesus. As a result, we reflect the lifestyles of those who become 'lovers of themselves, lovers of money, boastful, proud, abusive, disobedient to their parents, ungrateful, unholy, without love, unforgiving, slanderous, without self-control, brutal, not lovers of the good, treacherous, rash, conceited, lovers of pleasure rather than lovers of God' (2 Tim 3:2–4 NIV). It is salutary to remember that such characteristics, which reflect a world that is based on a self-centred expression of power, are describing people who are outwardly religious but inwardly bereft of God's power.

The power to be like Jesus

In essence, the resurrection power of Jesus is given to help us live like him. That is the nub of Paul's prayer for the Christians at Colossae.

> We pray this in order that you may live a life worthy of the Lord and may please him in every way: bearing fruit in every good work, growing in the knowledge of God, being strengthened with all power according to his glorious might so that you may have great endurance and patience. (Col 1:10–11 NIV)

It is this 'imitation of Christ' in the power of the Holy Spirit which permeates the writings of the New Testament (apart from the gospels). Paul several times urges his readers to imitate him in the way in which he imitates Christ (e.g. 1 Cor 11:1).

Nowhere is this point made more clearly than in the parting instructions of the risen Lord Jesus to his disciples prior to his ascension, instructions commonly known as 'the great commission' (Matt 28:18–20). First, he declares that 'all authority in heaven and on earth' has been given to him: in other words, by faithfully carrying through his ministry of laying out and laying down his life in obedience to his Father, he has inherited – and begun to possess – everything in heaven and on earth. The way of self-giving has been vindicated and has triumphed. Now he commissions his disciples to go and bring men and women ('all nations') into personal discipleship – 'teaching them to obey everything I have commanded you' (20, NIV). So, his example of and his message about cross-shaped discipleship became the manifesto of the church in every generation – 'to the very end of the age' (20, NIV), or this world as we know it. He promises his personal, unbroken presence to equip his disciples for this great commission: 'and lo, I am with you always'.

We cannot, therefore, afford to be selective in our imitation of Christ: he must be our complete model, both in what we do and say, and in the way we do and say it. As we have seen, it is in the matter of power that his model is so demonstrably different from all other human examples. This is not so much a question of key texts, as of the whole thrust and demeanour of his ministry. As the Holy Spirit daily fills us, we will increasingly imitate Jesus. At times we will be led by the Spirit into direct confrontation with the powers of darkness; that will lead to a power encounter, in which only the humble will see victory. At other times, the Spirit will inspire us to gifts of healings and to miracles. At all times, the Spirit will impress upon us more and more the call to be holy like Jesus and to be boldly compassionate in pointing men and women to Jesus.

Power in the early church

These four priorities – i.e. the power to bring deliverance from evil forces, the power to heal, the power to be holy, and the power to witness to Jesus as Lord – are plain in the way the first Christians imitated Jesus in the Acts of the Apostles. The power of Jesus was present with Peter, John and Stephen in their initial mission to the Jews. Equally, the power of Jesus was present with Philip in his mission to the Samaritans; it was also present with Paul, Barnabas, Silas, Titus, Timothy and others in their mission to the Gentiles. Peter's own summary of Jesus' ministry is an accurate synopsis of the way the Lord expressed his new life, directly in his three years in Galilee and Jerusalem, and indirectly through the Holy Spirit in the believers after Pentecost – 'God anointed Jesus of Nazareth with the Holy Spirit and with power . . . he went about doing good and healing all that were oppressed by the devil, for God was with him' (Acts 10:38).

God was with Jesus in the power of the Holy Spirit because he humbled himself and became obedient to his Father, learning this absolute obedience through the things which he suffered (cf. Heb 5:8). When Jesus died, it looked as if that way of divine power had been snuffed out and proved to be unrealistic, impossible in the harsh, self-centred, assertive world of human (and satanic) power. His resurrection proved such pessimism ill-founded: not even death could stop the power of God in the self-emptying of Jesus. 'Easter is not victory over the cross; it is the victory of the cross!'[5] Now Jesus is able to save completely those who come to God through him (cf. Heb 7:25) – how? 'By the power of an indestructible life' (Heb 7:16), a life of self-giving and ser-vanthood, which not even death on the cross could destroy. If death, 'the last enemy' (1 Cor 15:26), could not quench the new life of Jesus in the power of the Spirit, then no other enemy of God or humanity can do it.

But that last enemy has still to be eliminated. This is why there is always a two-edged reality in the death of a believer – and why this will remain so until death itself is finally des-troyed on 'the last day'. Henri Nouwen describes one of his own experiences in pastoral ministry in Peru, an experience which probably echoes our own encounters with Christian dying – its victory and its sorrow:

'There is one more thing I want you to do,' said Ann . . . 'There is a lady here who lost her only son of 16 years last month. His name was Walter. She wants you to go with her to the cemetery, pray with her, and bless the grave' . . . Ann and I drove with Walter's mother in the jeep to the small cemetery behind the hospital. There we found the little niche where Walter's body was laid. We prayed and I sprinkled the place with holy water and we cried . . . I couldn't keep my eyes from the woman's face, a gentle and deep face that had known much suffering. She had given birth to eight children: seven girls and Walter. When I stood in front of the grave, I had a feeling of powerlessness and a strong desire to call Walter back to life. 'Why can't I give Walter back to his mother?' I asked myself. But then I realized that my ministry lay more in powerlessness than in power: I could give her only my tears.[6]

The fiercest struggle will ensue wherever the strength of human power, in all its self-assertiveness, comes into conflict with the principle of self-giving ultimately fleshed out by Jesus on the cross. The more entrenched such human power has become in an individual, an organisation or a society, the more bitter will be the opposition when the message of the cross is accurately brought to bear. In the wisdom of God, this application of the cross to the powerful is most effectively done by those who are, in human terms, the weakest. That was certainly true of Jesus. It continues to be true today, because 'God chose the weak things of the world to shame the strong' (1 Cor 1:27 NIV).

Some false deductions

On that basis, it is misleading (because it is misled) to stress that only the influential and the powerful can reach the influential and the powerful: the precise opposite would appear to be the case. We need, rather, to search out ways and means of putting weak, insignificant people across the path of those who hold worldly power. There can be no avoiding the cost of bowing the knee to Jesus as Lord, especially in the matter of power. God fully determines that nobody should boast in his presence; he resists the proud, but gives grace to the humble. It is his grace in the humble which shames the proud and the powerful.

I am personally convinced that one of the most significant indications of God's grace at work in 'charismatic renewal' over the last twenty-five years has been in freeing Christians to get in touch with their weakness and their failures. There has been a much greater honesty, a readiness to share openly and be vulnerable. This tendency is, I believe, an authentic mark of God's Spirit bringing believers into alignment with the way and model of Jesus on the Calvary road. As a result, we have seen clearer evidence of the Spirit's new life flowing into worship, evangelism, practical ministry and – less pervasively but still significantly – involvement in the socio-political arena.

Because these are all immense benefits in the church today, it is particularly tragic when the fundamental authenticity of this new spiritual impetus becomes subtly contaminated by a creeping triumphalism. In essence, this attitude baptises human and worldly approaches to power and attempts to use them in the name of Christianity. Results and success become all-important; any means to those ends become legitimate. It becomes imperative that we should see things happen, rather than that the needs and sensitivities of individuals should be met with the compassion of Christ. God is perceived to be at work only when we can actually point to visible and tangible evidence along certain prescribed lines.

George MacDonald trenchantly exposed the dangers of trading exclusively in success when he wrote, 'In whatever man does without God, he must fail miserably – or succeed more miserably.'[7]

Money, marketing, methodology, manipulation and success: these are ingredients in our modern – indeed, in all worldly – exercise of power. It is easy for Christians uncritically to combine these with spiritual ingredients, such as faith, hope and joy. We add the triumphant aspects of our Christian faith to the ingredients of proven worldly success. The more I examine this trend, the more I form the conclusion that it has its origins in a faulty – or at least misleading – doctrine of the resurrection. This doctrine is not normally thought through and spelt out. It is assumed that Christians filled with the Spirit have somehow put the way of the cross behind them. The triumph of the resurrection is interpreted as having reversed the tragedy of the cross.

The story is told of Clarence Jordan, founder of Koinonia Farms, the first interracial community in the American South.

From its inception, this experiment in Christian community met with violent and bitter opposition from the (white) townspeople in nearby Americus, Georgia. Arson, beatings and death threats were among some of their more favourite ways of responding to Jordan and his enterprise. Soon everyone had been driven from the farm except Jordan and his family. Some of his buildings were in ashes and it appeared he would have to move. Someone asked him, grinning maliciously, 'Well, Clarence, just how successful do you think this whole thing has been?' Jordan thought for a moment and answered quietly, 'Oh, I guess it's been about as successful as the cross.'[8]

The cross as a way of life

The main thrust of this book, as will have become clearer chapter by chapter, is that by the resurrection God has eternally vindicated the way and the message of the cross. So, far from consigning the cross to one pivotal point in history (which it certainly is), God has in the resurrection of Jesus written the cross for all time and for eternity into the permanent experience of humanity – and by his Spirit he is continuously writing the cross into the daily lives of those who receive Jesus as Lord. The power of the resurrection, therefore, endorses the truth of the cross. Far from taking us beyond the cross, it plunges us into the cross – a journey and a commitment we could never face, except in the immeasurable power of One who has actually transcended even death itself. The cross without the resurrection presents us with the way of Jesus as a wonderful, but impossible, ideal; the cross *and* the resurrection together have brought into reality a whole new world, in which Jesus by his Spirit gradually recreates in us the way of the cross. Instead of snatching, grasping, grabbing our way to success and power, we are gradually freed to be generous, compassionate servants.

   This is why A. W. Tozer was right to warn that 'a new cross' had crept into Christianity, a cross that had little to do with suffering, sacrifice or death. 'The new cross does not slay the sinner', Tozer wrote: 'it redirects him. It gears him into a cleaner and jollier way of living and saves his self-respect'.[9]

Christ's finished work

When we begin to see the resurrection as a vindication, not a reversal, of the cross, we are also in a better position to appreciate the importance of seeing Christ's work of salvation as finished and completed once for all in his cross. In John's gospel this perspective is particularly clear, especially in the climactic cry of triumph from Jesus on the cross, 'It is finished' (John 19:30). Everything Jesus came from his Father to do for the salvation of mankind had been accomplished. Paul seems to interpret the significance of the cross in the same way: 'When you were dead in your sins . . . God made you alive with Christ. He forgave us all our sins . . . And having disarmed the powers and authorities, he made a public spectacle of them, triumphing over them by the cross' (Col 2:13–15 NIV). The triumph was complete in the cross. By raising Jesus from the dead, God vindicated his obedience even to death on the cross. God demonstrated in the resurrection that Christ's atoning work on behalf of mankind had been perfectly completed at the cross. The claims of Jesus about his identity and his mission were fully upheld by God: 'Jesus Christ our Lord' was 'through the spirit of holiness . . . declared with power to be the Son of God, by his resurrection from the dead' (Rom 1:4 NIV).

The new life to which Christians have been raised along with Jesus is, therefore, a life both marked by the cross and modelled in the cross. It is a life which death cannot touch, let alone terminate. It is a life in which we say no to ourselves and yes to our Father God. It is a life which is daily renewed in the Holy Spirit. It is a life full of new things, full of surprises, full of signs and wonders. It is a life with an absorbing purpose, the purpose of doing the will of God. It is the life of the kingdom of God, of the new world which was proclaimed in the ministry of Jesus. It is a life made universally accessible through the death of Jesus, inaugurated in the resurrection of Jesus, and personally entered and enjoyed as individuals are born again and are daily led by the Spirit of Jesus – life which will be fully consummated at the return of Jesus.

10   FINAL VINDICATION –
THE POWER AND THE GLORY

History is moving towards its climax in the return of Jesus Christ to the earth as judge and saviour – to save all those who eagerly wait for him (cf. Heb 9:28) and to execute judgment on all those who have refused to submit to him and obey him (cf. 2 Thess 1:8–9). The New Testament refers to this climax as taking place on a day which God has fixed (Acts 17:31). It is described, variously but consistently, as 'the day of the Lord Jesus' (2 Cor 1:14), 'the day of the Lord' (2 Thess 2:2), 'the day of Christ' (Phil 1:10; 2:16), 'the day of Jesus Christ (Phil 1:6) – or simply as 'the Day' (Heb 10:25), 'that Day' (2 Tim 4:8), or 'the great day' (Jude 6).

In essence, this day will mark the full unveiling of Jesus. No longer will anyone be under any illusions about his identity, his nature and his sovereignty. He will 'appear' so fully and so clearly, that we will 'see him as he is' (1 John 3:2). As far as his opponents are concerned, it will be 'the great day of their [God and his Lamb's] wrath' (Rev 6:17). As far as his worshippers are concerned, it is the day of 'our being gathered to him' (2 Thess 2:1 NIV). It is a day when ultimate and eternal distinctions will be made – 'When the Son of Man comes in his glory . . . he will sit on his glorious throne . . . Before him will be gathered all the nations, and he will separate them one from another as a shepherd separates the sheep from the goats' (Matt 25:31–32). The eternal destiny of the two groups is described by Jesus in terms of either eternal punishment or eternal life (Matt 25:46).

Jesus will be not only the agent of this judgment, but also the touchstone of this judgment – '[God] has fixed a day on which he will judge the world . . . by a man whom he has appointed' (Acts 17:31). It is the man Jesus of Nazareth to whom God has entrusted all judgment (cf. John 5:22). When he is fully revealed everyone will unmistakably recognise in him the perfect expression of divinity in a human being. In his vindication as the one in whom is vested all power and all authority, he will be recognised as having demonstrated that power in self-giving, serving, loving and laying down his life. When the disciples of Jesus are seen as also taking part in this judgment (cf. Matt 19:29; 1 Cor 6:2; Rev 20:4), we must assume that this will be the result of the impact of the Spirit's work in their lives, making them more and more like Jesus – i.e. servants who lay down their own lives in compassionate availability to others. They will substantially reinforce the right of Jesus to be judge.

The Lamb on the throne

Perhaps this is the essential impact of the amazing focus in the book of Revelation – a book as 'preoccupied with the problems of power'[1] as is our own age – on Jesus Christ as the Lamb who has been slain. When the apostle John, led by the Spirit, looked through heaven's open door to glimpse the heart of eternity, he was expecting to see 'the Lion of the tribe of Judah' on the throne (cf. Rev 5:5–6). What he actually saw was a Lamb, the symbol of vulnerability and weakness; and the Lamb bore the marks of slaughter, as a victim rather than a victor. Yet it was because of this vulnerability and this sacrifice that he had been launched on his triumphant reign. George Caird summarises this astounding perspective thus: 'Omnipotence is not to be understood as the power of unlimited coercion, but as . . . the invincible power of self-negating, self-sacrificing love.'[2]

When, therefore, we think of the returning Christ in his power and glory, we seem once again to be forced to re-examine what we are meant actually to expect. In rather similar fashion to the great reversal theory of the resurrection, we have usually taken on board an understanding of the second coming which anticipates a massive, unprecedented display of divine power. We accordingly tend to picture that great day as standing in stark contrast both to the relative obscurity of Christ's earthly life and to the steady, but basically unspectacular, spread of the gospel since Pentecost. When the day of the Lord dawns, we feel sure it will be utterly different: no more weakness, hiddenness, vulnerability; no more serving or self-humbling; no more giving your life away – but wearing the crown and sitting on the throne.

The New Testament clearly uses such language. But we still need to ask what kind of power and authority it is describing. Crowns and thrones are only pictures of reality. If it is true that Jesus, the eternal Son of God, saw Godlikeness, his divinity, in terms of not snatching, grabbing and manipulating – or, more positively, in terms of giving, loving and serving – then it is virtually impossible to imagine that he ever has seen or ever will see it in any other way. He is 'the same yesterday and today and for ever' (Heb 13:8); he is hardly likely to change his approach to power at the very moment of his full vindication. When he is revealed in his true identity, he will be revealed as the one who emptied himself and humbled himself. That is what God is like: that is what Jesus is like. George Caird put it like this, 'When Jesus spoke of the glory of the Son of Man, he was predicting not so much his own personal victory as the triumph of the cause he served.'[3]

A number of New Testament perspectives on the day of the Lord substantiate this understanding of 'the last things'. Perhaps the most striking is the attitude which will apparently motivate Jesus when he assumes universal sovereignty. In Paul's vivid language it is put like this: 'Then the end will come, when he [Christ] hands over the kingdom to God the Father after he has destroyed all dominion, authority and power' (1 Cor 15:24 NIV). These last three terms are shorthand for every exercise and manifestation of power in any way opposed to God and contrary to his will – whether by human beings, angels, demons or Satan. Since the resurrection, Jesus has been gradually asserting his reign over all these powers. On that final day he will fully triumph, having 'rendered utterly ineffective' (literal meaning of 'destroyed') every other power.

How Jesus will exercise his supreme power

What will Jesus then do with his universal sovereignty? If that climax to history is to be the grand reversal to end all grand reversals, we would expect him then to assert his proper authority as King of kings and Lord of lords. Instead, Paul's language encourages us to see Jesus gladly handing over his sovereignty to God the Father. He will then be acting entirely in character, i.e. not holding on to what he could (in human reckoning) legitimately claim to be his own by right of suffering and death. Instead of grasping total sovereignty, he gives it away – because that is what God is like, has always been like, and will for ever be like. So eternally committed is the Son of God to this kind of self-giving, that 'the Son himself will be made subject to him who put everything under him, so that God may be all in all' (1 Cor 15:28 NIV). Because the nature of God is to give, we can be sure that he will not contradict himself when he is 'all in all'.

Another insight into the essential and eternal nature of Jesus, as it will be made universally plain on that great day, is given in an astounding passage in Luke's gospel, Luke 12:35–40. Jesus is here teaching his disciples about the need for watchfulness, 'because the Son of Man will come at an hour when you do not expect him' (Luke 12:40 NIV). The instructions begin, 'Be dressed ready for service' (Luke 12:35 NIV). The passage then appears to interweave parable and metaphor. In the parable, Jesus describes his disciples as being 'like men waiting for their master to return from a wedding banquet' (Luke 12:36 NIV). He urges them to be ready to open the door to him, whatever time he returns. Then he turns the picture upside down. Instead of the master disappearing to bed for a good sleep, 'he will dress himself to serve, will have them recline at the table and will come and wait on them' (Luke 12:37 NIV). He stresses the striking truth of this by the introductory phrase – 'verily, I say unto you' (Luke 12:37 AV).

We have, therefore, in this parable the amazing picture of the triumphant Lord Jesus Christ, returning in power and great glory, and stripping himself to wait on his disciples, to be a servant, or (more literally) a deacon. There could hardly be a more evocative or explicit foreshadowing of the scene in the upper room, when Jesus took a towel and washed the disciples' feet. He will, apparently, be doing the same humble service when he is revealed as Lord of lords and King of kings. If we are going to talk about reversals of role, this is the greatest of all – and yet, paradoxically, it will be completely in character, because the power of God has consistently been revealed in such humble serving and such generous giving.

Serving in heaven

A further striking aspect of the events on that great day is consistently suggested by the frequent motif of servants, both in the parables of Jesus about his return and in the vision of heaven in the book of Revelation. However strong the New Testament emphasis on believers being the children of God, friends not servants, both these portions of the New Testament seem consciously to identify God's people as his servants. This is best summarised in the final vision of John about the new Jerusalem (Revelation 21–22), particularly in the fitting paradox of 22:3–5 (NIV) – 'his servants will serve him . . . And they will reign for ever and ever.'

Servants who reign present an immediate contradiction. It has been traditionally taught that God's servants will share in the triumphant dominion of the Lord himself. If, however, Jesus exercises his power consistently in humble service and if this behaviour is not reversed but reinforced when his kingly rule is consummated, then his servants will continue to serve in heaven – and the greatest in the kingdom of heaven will eternally be the one who is the truest servant of all (cf. Matt 18:1–4; 20:20–28). By that stage, all pursuers and perpetrators of worldly power will have been eliminated from the sphere of God's sovereignity (cf. Rev 21:27; 22:15). Only those will be inside the city of God who have humbled themselves to *receive* 'the free gift of the water of life' (Rev 21:6; 22:17 NIV).

The final destruction of unrestrained lawlessness

It seems – from the teaching of several passages in the New Testament – that the unveiling on that day of Jesus and the true nature of his power will be preceded by an unprecedented build-up of all that is worst in worldly power. The full and final judgment of the Lord Jesus will be directed at this concentration of worldly power. For example, Paul writes like this:

> that day will not come until the rebellion occurs and the man of lawlessness is revealed, the man doomed to destruction. He will oppose and will exalt himself over everything that is called God or is worshipped, so that he sets himself up in God's temple, proclaiming himself to be God.
>
> (2 Thess 2:3–4 NIV)

Paul recognises that 'the secret power of lawlessness is already at work' (2 Thess 2:7 NIV), but that there is a significant measure of restraint on its impact and activity. Otherwise, presumably, society in general would completely disintegrate. In the latter part of the twentieth century we certainly have reason to accept the credibility of such a perspective on the world. At times, it feels as if all we need is one more tidal wave of violence for the dam to collapse.

We are assured by Paul that the world will not ultimately end in an uncontrolled orgy of destruction – such a scenario is only penultimate, not final. The forces of violence, lawlessness, rebelliousness, arrogance, greed and idolatry will certainly increase. They will reach the point where all restraints will be removed and any veneer of attractiveness will be stripped away. The revelation of evil will be as complete as the revelation of Jesus – the same word, 'apocalypse', is used of both events. The path of power originally chosen by Satan, and followed by humanity since the fall, will be made uninhibitedly plain. But what will happen when 'the lawless one will be revealed'? 'The Lord Jesus will overthrow [him] with the breath of his mouth and destroy [him] by the splendour of his coming' (2 Thess 2:8 NIV). He will not need anything by way of weapons or instruments. He will not use force or violence. He will demonstrate his complete victory simply by his appearance and his word. That is all Jesus has ever needed to demonstrate his power. To be present and to speak, that is the essence of the power of Jesus.

This simple secret of divine power becomes even more significant in the light of Paul's description of what will happen when defiant lawlessness is rampant.

> The coming of the lawless one will be in accordance with the work of Satan displayed in all kinds of counterfeit miracles, signs and wonders, and in every sort of evil that deceives those who are perishing. They perish because they refused to love the truth and so be saved. (2 Thess 2:9–10 NIV)

We can only begin to imagine the bedlam and the horror of those days leading up to the day of the Lord. The unrestrained violence, destructiveness and cruelty of human power will be indescribable, both for its ghastliness and for its sheer effectiveness.

A nuclear holocaust?

Something of its appalling impact is now accessible to us in our life under the threat of a nuclear holocaust. The matter now at stake is the survival of our world; the power now in question is 'the most transcendent power of all – the power to end all other exercises of power'.[4] Those involved in the production of nuclear arms 'almost casually assume and defend the power to arbitrate and control the question of the survival of the human race'.[5] Those who question these experts, who have become 'theologically adjusted to the concept of mass-death',[6] are deemed to be unqualified to speak on such a subject. This becomes even more remarkable when we recall that 'the nearest the modern general or admiral comes to a small-arms encounter of any sort is at a duck-hunt in the company of corporation executives at the retreat of Continental Motors, Inc.'[7]

Yet, however immense this massive escalation of destructive power, that is precisely the moment when Jesus will come, will speak, will silence and destroy. He will come as the Truth: he will declare his word of truth, the truth of the gospel, the message of the cross.

The scene is nowhere better described than in the book of Revelation:

> Then the kings of the earth, the princes, the generals, the rich, the mighty, and every slave and every free man hid in caves and among the rocks of the mountains. They called to the mountains and the rocks, 'Fall on us and hide us from the face of him who sits on the throne and from the wrath of the Lamb! For the great day of their wrath has come, and who can stand?' (Rev 6:15–17 NIV)

It is, of course, impossible for any human language to describe the awesome events to take place on that climactic day. It is not surprising that Paul describes it as the time 'when the Lord Jesus is revealed from heaven in blazing fire' (2 Thess 1:7 NIV). After all, 'our God is a consuming fire' (Heb 12:29). But the image of fire ought not to divert us from the essential nature of God as holy love. When the Lord Jesus is revealed from heaven, he will be revealed as the God of holy love. We will see him then to be such a God: we will recognise that everything we had hitherto known of him was but a brief, distant glimpse of his holy love. That kind of life to which he now, by his Spirit, inspires us – a life of compassionate service and humble obedience – will be written perfectly into us in the fullness of his eternal kingdom. He will continue into eternity as our model and our inspiration, the major difference being that then 'we shall be like him, for we shall see him as he is' (1 John 3:2).

The basis of divine judgment

It stands to reason, therefore, that the basis of judgment on that day will be our response to Jesus in terms of receiving the message of the cross and expressing the way of the cross. That is the thrust of the teaching about the sheep and the goats. It is a message about our fundamental approach to people, especially the weak and the powerless – i.e. how we use our power with others, the power given by possessing food and drink, the power that comes from enjoying good health and many personal freedoms, the power which has a home of our own and space to spare, the power of having more than we personally need by way of clothing and daily bread.

Do we hold on to these good things, regarding them as our right and going after more? Is our attitude one of grabbing, grasping and snatching? Do we use our possessions and our power to control people, to bring them round to our wishes, to increase our own comfort and happiness? Are people there for our convenience and to boost our own image and reputation? Jesus is looking for those who, like himself, give away what they have to those who have not and who cannot repay in kind. He wants people who share, serve and show compassion. The call to serve was entirely clear even to 'the goats' in the story: when challenged by Jesus for not doing what mattered, they replied, 'Lord, when did we see thee hungry or thirsty or a stranger or naked or sick or in prison, and did not *minister* to thee?' (Matt 25:44). The word minister is, again, the one which means 'to be a deacon'. They knew in their consciences the force of the divine call to serve, but they had stifled it.

In both our daily lives and on the day of judgment, therefore, Jesus comes to us with an identical challenge. He comes as the one who has humbled himself and who continues to humble himself to be present among us in the weak and the powerless. On our response to this Jesus depends whether we receive or forfeit our inheritance, 'the kingdom prepared for [us] since the creation of the world' (Matt 25:34 NIV). To align ourselves in this world with Jesus is to stand critically apart from, and often to fly in the face of, the power structures and power priorities which hold sway around us. Such alignment with Jesus will actually attract the hostility of those with vested interests in retaining power. Can we retain faith in the God and Father of our Lord Jesus Christ when we are thus opposed and rejected? That was the question Jesus himself put about his second coming: 'When the Son of Man comes, will he find faith on earth?' – in the context (Luke 18:1–8), that refers to faith in a righteous God, who will see that those on the receiving end of an unjust use of power will ultimately receive justice.

How we live today

This brings us face to face with the direct question: in what way does our belief about the ultimate future affect the way we live today? The simple answer is: radically. If we have developed convictions about God's kingdom in heaven which focus on exercising authority and power over others, then we will be looking for glimpses and foretastes of that in our everyday life now. One group sees this as bringing that eternal future into the present in terms of prosperity, healing, victory, etc. Another group sees the kingdom of God essentially in terms of justice and equality; it too strives to project such a society into the present as fully as possible.

It may well be, also, that similar factors are at work among those Christians who believe in a literal thousand years' reign on earth by Christ, together with his servants (cf. Rev 20:1–6), before the final day of the Lord. The relevant passage in Revelation 20, if it is to be taken this literally, refers to such a situation being entrusted to 'those who had been beheaded for their testimony to Jesus' (Rev 20:4) (presumably a fairly limited number). Is such an item of faith ('We will all be ruling in Moscow') the result of an understandable, but unbiblical, desire on the part of those with little worldly power to see the roles reversed and to enjoy being important? In other words, the basic desire for power in our unredeemed, or certainly unsanctified, hearts is legitimised on the basis of a disputed article of belief.

If, on the other hand, the fullness of God's kingly rule will see Jesus revealed unmistakably as eternal deacon, humbling himself and giving himself in compassionate service for others, then this will be the inspiration and the pattern which moulds those here and now who have bowed the knee to Jesus as suffering servant and – therefore – as Lord. God has 'set eternity in the hearts of men' (Eccl 3:11): the shape and the substance which we give to this sense of eternity in our hearts must inevitably affect our daily lives.

End-time priorities

When Peter was as yet uncontrolled by the Spirit of Jesus, he was classically driven by the methods and goals of worldly power. When he had been gradually transformed by the Spirit, he saw Christian priorities very differently, especially in the light of the return of Jesus. When constrained to write that 'the end of all things is at hand', he urged three priorities on his readers as expressions of clearheadedness in such a crisis – love, give, serve (cf. 1 Pet 4:7–11). Peter could see then what he could not see when Jesus was alive in the flesh – that only thus is God praised through Jesus Christ. Stephen Neill has written: 'If we see God in Jesus Christ, what is the principal thing that we learn about him? It is that God is a servant, and that, when he most fully makes himself the servant of all, the glory of his power finds its fullest self-expression.'[8]

In a similar way, when Paul is concluding his pastoral advice to young Timothy and directing his thinking towards 'the appearing of our Lord Jesus Christ' (1 Tim 6:11–19), the priorities he stresses are significant. As far as necessary qualities of character are concerned, Paul urges Timothy to pursue 'righteousness, godliness, faith, love, steadfastness' (1 Tim 6:11) – all qualities which we would expect an older and a wiser man to spotlight. He adds a striking quality to the list – the Greek word is *praupatheia*, meekness. This is the quality which we noted earlier in the character of Jesus, signifying a person who has learnt to submit, whose power is under the control of someone else – like a tamed animal. Such proper meekness is the essential ingredient of a life committed to love, to give and to serve, rather than to snatch, to grab and to dominate. Paul wants Timothy to pursue such meekness.

Paul actually points to Jesus' example before Pontius Pilate as the perfect model for the young man's daily witness. Such meekness certainly has no connotation of passivity, because Paul insists that it involves hot pursuit and fighting 'the good fight of the faith' (1 Tim 6:12); it means taking a firm hold on the life of God as given in and through Jesus. Timothy will meet many powerful men of the world, people with influence, authority and immense resources at their disposal. He must remind himself and them that there is only one Ruler, only one King, only one Lord. He alone is worthy of praise, honour and might for eternity. Such wealthy and – in a worldly sense – powerful people must be told firmly not to put their trust in uncertain riches and not to become arrogant or dismissive of others. Instead, they must place their trust uninhibitedly in God, the provider of all good things, and accordingly develop a lifestyle which is rich in generosity and in sharing. In this way they, too, show that they have authentically aligned themselves with Jesus, God's gift to us beyond words (2 Cor 9:15), who 'though he was rich, yet for [our] sakes . . . became poor, so that [we] through his poverty might become rich' (2 Cor 8:9 NIV).

> No one had been more tempted than Jesus to seize and use worldly power . . . But in every temptation Jesus chose the other way, the way of faithfulness to the Father's will, the way of the Cross . . . He used almighty power to take upon Himself the form of a lowly and humble servant . . . He stooped to enter into the heart of the world's sin and deal it a death-blow by atoning sacrifice. It was as such . . . that He descended to enter a world under the sway of principalities and powers, to strike at . . . the proud ego of a humanity that desires to be as God, and to emancipate men from the bondage of their own guilt to the freedom of Truth and Love.[9]

God's training for eternity

While we remain on this earth, God by his Spirit is working in us the demeanour and the behaviour of Jesus, i.e. patiently preparing us for the life of heaven, which will be spent in eternal servanthood after the model of Jesus. We all find it painful to be called to serve others, because of our rebellious, self-indulgent natures. In the perfection of heaven we will rejoice to serve one another and to serve God. Every painful, awkward and humbling experience now is part of God's training for eternity.

A London restaurateur recently drew an unfavourable comparison between his English waiters and those from most other European countries, as well as from Asia. English waiters see their job as a chore; most others enjoy it. The English do not like to serve, he remarked; they see it as beneath their dignity. Other nationalities, he concluded, are glad to bring satisfaction and pleasure to people; they see their serving as an opportunity to make others happier. It may be that English Christians find the serving motif equally painful and humbling.

To conclude, we can do no better than quote in full the passage from Philippians 2:1–11 (GNB) which has been at the heart of this book's message:

> Your life in Christ makes you strong, and his love comforts you. You have fellowship with the Spirit, and you have kindness and compassion for one another. I urge you, then, to make me completely happy by having the same thoughts, sharing the same love, and being one in soul and mind. Don't do anything from selfish ambition or from a cheap desire to boast, but be humble towards one another, always considering others better than yourselves. And look out for one another's interests, not just for your own. The attitude you should have is the one that Christ Jesus had:
>
> He always had the nature of God,
>> but he did not think that by force he should try to remain[10] equal with God.
> Instead of this, of his own free will he gave up all he had,
>> and took the nature of a servant.
> He became like man
>> and appeared in human likeness.
> He was humble and walked the path of obedience all the way to death –
>> his death on the cross.
> For this reason God raised him to the highest place above
>> and gave him the name that is greater than any other name.
> And so, in honour of the name of Jesus
>> all beings in heaven, on earth, and in the world below will fall on their knees,
> and all will openly proclaim that Jesus Christ is Lord,
>> to the glory of God the Father.

NOTES

Introduction

1 Tacitus,
2 Friedrich Nietzsche,
3 Bertrand Russell,
4 J. K. Galbraith,
5 John F. Kennedy,
6 William Hazlitt,
7 Bertrand de Jouvenal,
8 Paul Tournier,
9 ibid.,
10 Albert Nolan, *Jesus Before Christianity* (Darton, Longman & Todd 1977).
11 John Stek,
12 Blaise Pascal,

1 Weak and helpless – the power of a baby

1 Many writers have questioned the historical content and accuracy of the infancy narratives in Matthew and Luke. For a full discussion, leading to a basically sceptical conclusion, see Raymond Brown, *The Birth of the Messiah* (Geoffrey Chapman 1977). For a cogent rebuttal of such scepticism, see Donald Carson, 'Matthew' in Frank E. Gaebelein (ed.), *The Expositor's Bible Commentary* 8 (Zondervan 1984), pp. 60–98.
2 'The history of Messianism is complex. In pre-exilic Israelite history, when there was an anointed king of the House of David (and thus a messiah) reigning in Jerusalem, hopes for deliverance from enemies or catastrophe were attached to that monarch. If he was bad, these hopes were attached to his successor . . . However, when the Babylonian exile of 587–539 BC brought an end to the reigning Davidic monarchy, and when in the early post-exilic period the dreams centered around

Zerubbabel . . . came to nought, the expectations surrounding the anointed kings of the House of David shifted to an anointed king of the indefinite future. And thus hope was born in *the* Messiah, the supreme anointed one who would deliver Israel', Brown, *Birth of the Messiah*, p. 67, note 9.

3 See the temporary phenomena mentioned by Gamaliel in Acts 5: 36–37.
4 Alfred Plummer, *An Exegetical Commentary on the Gospel According to St Matthew* (Robert Scott 1909), p. 12.
5 A full translation of the Eclogue can be found in Brown, *Birth of the Messiah*, pp. 566–567.
6 Carson, 'Matthew', p. 85.
7 Plummer, *St Matthew*, pp. 13–14.
8 John Calvin, *Commentary on a Harmony of the Evangelists, Matthew, Mark, and Luke* (Eerdmans 1949), p. 136.
9 Walter Liefeld, 'Luke' in Frank Gaebelein (ed.), *The Expositor's Bible Commentary* 8 (Zondervan 1984), p. 845.
10 Brown, *Birth of the Messiah*, p. 429.
11 Liefeld, 'Luke', p. 845.
12 Plummer, *St Matthew*, p. 249.
13 Henri Nouwen, *Gracias* (Harper & Row 1984), p. 15.
14 Donald Guthrie, *New Testament Theology* (IVP 1981), p. 348.
15 Nouwen, *Gracias*, p. 62.

2 Taking the easy way – power struggle

1 Leon Morris, *The Gospel According to St Luke* The Tyndale New Testament Commentaries (IVP 1974), p. 102.
2 Alfred Plummer, *An Exegetical Commentary on the Gospel According to St Matthew* (Robert Scott 1909), p. 35.
3 Donald Carson, 'Matthew' in Frank Gaebelein, *The Expositor's Bible Commentary* 8 (Zondervan 1984), p. 111.
4 Donald Guthrie, *New Testament Theology* (IVP 1981), p. 222 n. 5.
5 Carson, 'Matthew', p. 112.
6 Plummer, *St Matthew*, p. 39.
7 ibid., p. 40.
8 Carson, 'Matthew', p. 113.
9 Calvin, *Commentary on a Harmony of the Evangelists, Matthew, Mark, and Luke* 1 (Eerdmans 1949), p. 219.
10 ibid.

11 R. T. France, *Jesus and the Old Testament* (Tyndale Press 1971), p. 52.
12 Plummer, *St Matthew*, p. 42.
13 Guthrie, *NT Theology*, p. 126.
14 ibid., p. 127.
15 Michael Griffiths has written more fully on the central importance of this *imitatio Christi* in *The Example of Jesus* (Hodder & Stoughton 1985).
16 As far as I am aware, Os Guinness has not yet made these observations in print, but they have been voiced during various lecture tours in the USA.

3 Such people are dangerous – power under control

1 Segundo Galilea, *The Beatitudes* (Orbis Books 1984), p. 9.
2 Under this and the next heading I have taken the liberty of modifying the RSV quotations: I have consistently used the word 'meek' or 'meekness' to render the Greek word *prautés* or *prautētos* where the RSV uses 'gentle' (Matt 11:29; 1 Pet 3:4), 'humble' (Zech 9:9) or 'gentleness' (2 Tim 2:25; 1 Pet 3:15; Gal 6:1; 1 Cor 4:21).
3 A story related in Cheryl Forbes, *The Religion of Power* (MARC Europe 1986), p. 34 and Richard Foster, *Money, Sex and Power* (Hodder & Stoughton 1985), p. 205, which indicates that Solzhenitsyn records it in his *Gulag Archipelago*.
4 Galilea, *The Beatitudes*, pp. 9, 11.
5 Donald Carson, 'Matthew' in Frank E. Gaebelein, *The Expositor's Bible Commentary* 8 (Zondervan 1984), p. 174.

4 Don't crowd me – power with his friends

1 According to Josephus (*Antiquities* 8. 119. 2), John was imprisoned in the notoriously grim fortress of Machaerus, east of the Dead Sea.
2 Donald Carson, 'Matthew' in Frank E. Gaebelein, *The Expositor's Bible Commentary* 8 (Zondervan 1984), pp. 265–268.
3 ibid., p. 267.
4 ibid.
5 ibid., p. 268.
6 ibid.
7 ibid., p. 277.

8   The Greek text here includes the word 'behind', and this is additional to the instruction to Satan in the wilderness. The word also occurs in Jesus' initial call to the disciples (including Peter) to follow him (Mark 1:17): i.e. 'follow *behind* me'. It is possible that Jesus is, therefore, reminding Peter of the right place for a true disciple – behind him, following; not in front of him, rebuking.

5   Who cares for the downtrodden? – power and the powerless

1   Segundo Galilea, *The Beatitudes* (Orbis Books 1984), pp. 14–15, 19.
2   Albert Nolan, *Jesus Before Christianity* (DLT 1977), p. 33.
3   For a concise examination of the theory, see Donald Guthrie, *New Testament Theology* (IVP 1981), pp. 238–243.
4   Donald Carson, 'Matthew' in Frank E. Gaebelein, *The Expositor's Bible Commentary* 8 (Zondervan 1984), p. 199.

6   The possessed – the power of money

1   J. K. Galbraith, *The Anatomy of Power* (Houghton Mifflin 1983), p. 50, my italics.
2   Jacques Ellul, *Money and Power* (IVP 1984), p. 43.
3   ibid., p. 68.
4   ibid., pp. 70–72.
5   ibid., p. 72.
6   ibid., p. 76
7   Donald Carson, 'Matthew' in Frank E. Gaebelein, *The Expositor's Bible Commentary* 8 (Zondervan 1984), p. 179.
8   Ellul, *Money and Power*, p. 84.
9   ibid., p. 86.
10 ibid., pp. 78–79.
11 ibid.
12 ibid., p. 87, my italics.
13 ibid., p. 88.
14 ibid., p. 110.
15 ibid., p. 112.
16 ibid., pp. 111–112.
17 ibid., p. 91.
18 ibid., p. 102.

7 The guardians of tradition – religious power

1 Leon Morris, *The Gospel According to John* The New International Commentary on the New Testament (Eerdmans 1971), p. 131.
2 William Barclay, *The Daily Study Bible: The Gospel of Matthew* 2 (St Andrew Press 1976), p. 282.
3 ibid., p. 285.
4 Although this incident is in print, it would be invidious to give either the reference or the pastor's name here.

8 Don't rock the boat – political power

1 Albert Nolan, *Jesus Before Christianity* (Darton, Longman & Todd 1977), p. 68.
2 G. Campbell Morgan, *The Gospel According to John* (Marshall, Morgan and Scott 1933), p. 284.
3 Segundo Galilea, *The Beatitudes* (Orbis Books 1984).
4 J. H. Yoder, *The Politics of Jesus* (Eerdmans 1972), p. 62, note 5.
5 Tacitus, *Histories* 5.9 and *Annals* 12.54 respectively.
6 Leon Morris, *The Gospel According to John* New International Commentary on the New Testament (Eerdmans 1971), p. 769.
7 Martin Luther King, cited in Richard Gregg, *The Power of Non-Violence* (Schocken Books 1971), p. 150.
8 Paul Tournier,
9 'Necklacing' is a method employed particularly in South Africa, by which a rubber tyre is placed around a suspect and then set on fire.
10 Yoder, *Politics of Jesus*, pp. 147–148.
11 ibid.
12 ibid.
13 ibid.

9 Victory and Freedom – resurrection power

1 Georges Casalis, in Jose Miguez Bonino (ed.), *Faces of Jesus: Latin American Christologies* (Orbis Books 1984), p. 76.
2 Saúl Trinidad, in Bonino (ed.), *Faces of Jesus*, p. 66, quoting Ricardo Rojas.
3 ibid., p. 60.
4 Casalis, in Bonino (ed.), *Faces of Jesus*, p. 74. (In fact I have

rearranged the sentences; in the original, the second sentence precedes the first and is on pp. 73–74.)
5   ibid., p. 75.
6   Henri Nouwen, *Gracias* (Harper & Row 1984), p. 91.
7   George MacDonald.
8   The story about Clarence Jordan is related in
9   A. W. Tozer.

10   Final vindication – the power and the glory

1   Leon Morris, *The Revelation of St John* The Tyndale New Testament Commentaries (Tyndale Press 1969), p. 13.
2   George Caird, *The Revelation of St John the Divine* Black's New Testament Commentaries (A. & C. Black 1966), p. 75.
3   ibid.
4   J. K. Galbraith, *The Anatomy of Power* (Houghton Mifflin 1983), pp. 167–168.
5   ibid.
6   ibid.
7   C. Wright Mills, *The Power Elite* (Oxford University Press 1956), p. 189.
8   Stephen Neill, *Crises of Belief* (Hodder & Stoughton 1984), p. 26.
9   Thomas Torrance, *The Apocalypse Today* (James Clarke 1960), pp. 91–92.
10 Following the GNB alternative reading, see chapter one for the reason for this choice.

BIBLIOGRAPHY

Bold numbers refer to chapters in *Jesus and Power* where a particular book is directly relevant to that chapter. The other books are useful for background, for biblical exegesis or for general illumination on the subject of power.

C. K. Barrett, *The Gospel According to St John* (SPCK 1978)

Leonardo Boff, *Jesus Christ Liberator* (Orbis Books 1978)

Jose Miguez Bonino (ed.), *Faces of Jesus: Latin American Christologies* (Orbis Books 1984)

Raymond E. Brown, *The Birth of the Messiah* (Geoffrey Chapman 1977), **1**

G. B. Caird, *The Revelation of St John the Divine* (A. & C. Black 1966)

G. B. Caird, *Saint Luke* The Pelican Gospel Commentaries (Penguin Books 1963)

Anthony Campolo, *The Power Delusion* (Victor Books 1983), **3**, **6** and **7**

Ernesto Cardenal, *The Gospel in Solentiname*, 4 vols (Orbis Books 1982)

Donald A. Carson, 'Matthew' in Frank E. Gaebelein (ed.), *The Expositor's Bible Commentary* 8 (Zondervan 1984)

Richard Cassidy, *Jesus, Politics and Society* (Orbis Books 1978), **5** and **8**

Richard Cassidy and Philip Scharper (eds), *Political Issues in Luke–Acts* (Orbis Books 1983), **8**

Jose Comblin, *Jesus of Nazareth* (Orbis Books 1976)

Orlando Costas, *The Integrity of Mission* (Harper & Row 1979)

C. E. B. Cranfield, *Saint Mark* (Cambridge University Press 1959)

Oscar Cullmann, *The Christology of the New Testament* (SCM Press 1959)

Oscar Cullmann, *Jesus and the Revolutionaries* **2** and **8**

John D'Ansbro, *Martin Luther King, Jr: The Making of a Mind* (Orbis Books 1982)

James D. G. Dunn, *Jesus and the Spirit* (SCM Press 1975)

James D. G. Dunn, *Christology in the Making* (SCM Press 1980)

Hugo Echegaray, *The Practice of Jesus* (Orbis Books 1984), **5** and **6**

Jacques Ellul, *Money and Power* (Inter-Varsity Press 1984), **6**

Cheryl Forbes, *The Religion of Power* (MARC Europe 1986), **2**, **6** and **7**

Richard Foster, *Celebration of Discipline* (Hodder & Stoughton 1980), **2**, **3** and **6**

Richard Foster, *The Freedom of Simplicity* (SPCK 1981), **1**, **5** and **6**

Richard Foster, *Money, Sex and Power* (Hodder & Stoughton 1985), **3**, **4**, **6** and **8**

J. K. Galbraith, *The Anatomy of Power* (Houghton Mifflin 1983)

Richard Gregg, *The Power of Non-Violence* (Schocken Books 1971)

Michael Green, *The Empty Cross of Jesus* (Hodder & Stoughton 1984)

Michael Griffiths, *The Example of Jesus* (Hodder & Stoughton 1985)

Donald Guthrie, *New Testament Theology* (Inter-Varsity Press 1981)

Gustavo Gutierrez, *We Drink From Our Own Wells* (Orbis Books 1984), **5**

Michael Harper, *The Healings of Jesus* (Hodder & Stoughton 1986), **4** and **5**

Martin Hengel, *Christ and Power* (Fortress Press 1977)

E. M. Howse, *Saints in Politics – The Clapham Sect and the Growth of Freedom* (George Allen & Unwin 1971), **5**, **6** and **8**

Joachim Jeremias, *Jerusalem in the Time of Jesus* (SCM Press 1969)

E. Stanley Jones, *Gandhi – Portrayal by a Friend* (Abingdon Press 1948)

Martin Luther King Jr, *The Trumpet of Conscience* (Harper & Row 1967)

Martin Luther King Jr., *Where Do We Go From Here?* (Harper & Row 1967)

George E. Ladd, *I Believe in the Resurrection of Jesus* (Hodder & Stoughton)

Walter L. Liefeld, 'Luke' in Frank E. Gaebelein (ed.) *The Expositor's Bible Commentary* 8 (Zondervan 1984)

I. Howard Marshall, *The Acts of the Apostles* (Inter-Varsity Press 1983)

I. Howard Marshall, *The Gospel of Luke* (Paternoster Press 1978)

I. Howard Marshall, *The Origins of New Testament Christology* (Inter-Varsity Press 1976)

Dom Moraes, *Indira Gandhi* (Little, Brown 1980)

Leon Morris, *The Gospel According to John* (William B. Eerdmans 1971)

Leon Morris, *Revelation* (Tyndale Press 1969)

C. F. D. Moule, *The Origin of Christology* (Cambridge University Press 1977)

Stephen Neill, *Crisis of Belief* (Hodder & Stoughton 1984)

Stephen Neill, *The Supremacy of Jesus* (Hodder & Stoughton 1983)

Friedrich Nietzsche, *The Will to Power* (Vintage Books 1968)

Albert Nolan, *Jesus Before Christianity* (Darton, Longman & Todd 1977)

Henri Nouwen, *Gracias* (Harper & Row 1984), 1 and 5

Oliver O'Donovan, *Resurrection and Moral Order* (Inter-Varsity Press 1986)

John Perkins, *Quiet Revolution* (Marshall, Morgan & Scott 1985)

Carl Rogers, *A Way of Being* (Houghton Mifflin 1980)

Edward Schillebeeckx, *Jesus* (Collins 1979)

Herbert Schlossberg, *Idols for Destruction* (Nelson 1983), 6, 7, and 8

H. J. Schultz (ed.), *Jesus in His Time* (Fortress Press 1971)

David Sheppard, *Bias to the Poor* (Hodder & Stoughton 1983), 5, 6 and 7

Ronald J. Sider, *Rich Christians in an Age of Hunger* (Hodder & Stoughton 1977), 2, 5 and 6

Tom Skinner, *Words of Revolution* (Paternoster Press 1971), 2 and 5

C. P. Snow, *The Corridors of Power* (Penguin Books 1951)

C. P. Snow, *The Masters* (Penguin Books 1951)

Jon Sobrino, *Christology at the Crossroads* (Orbis Books 1978)

Thomas F. Torrance, *The Apocalypse Today* (James Clarke 1960)

Paul Tournier, *The Strong and the Weak* (SCM Press 1963), 5

Paul Tournier, *The Violence Inside* (SCM Press 1978), 3

Geza Vermes, *Jesus the Jew* (Collins Fontana 1976)

Jim Wallis, *Agenda for Biblical People* (Harper & Row 1976), 5, 6 and 7

Jim Wallis, *Call to Conversion* (Lion Publishing), 3, 5 and 6

W. W. Wessel, 'Mark' in Frank E. Gaebelein (ed.), *The Expositor's Bible Commentary* 8 (Zondervan 1984)

John Howard Yoder, *The Politics of Jesus* (William B. Eerdmans 1972), 2, 5 and 8